Published by Quintessentially Publishing Ltd.
10 Carlisle Street
London W1D 3BR
Tel: +44 (0)845 224 7419
Fax: +44 (0)207 692 0213

Email (for orders and customer service enquiries)
quintessentiallyperfume@quintessentially.com

Visit us at: www.quintessentiallypublishing.com

ISBN 9780955827068
Printed and bound in the UK by Solutions In Ink Limited.

Design by:
Quintessentially Design Ltd.
10 Carlisle Street
London W1D 3BR
Tel: +44 (0)207 758 3331
www.quintessentiallydesign.com

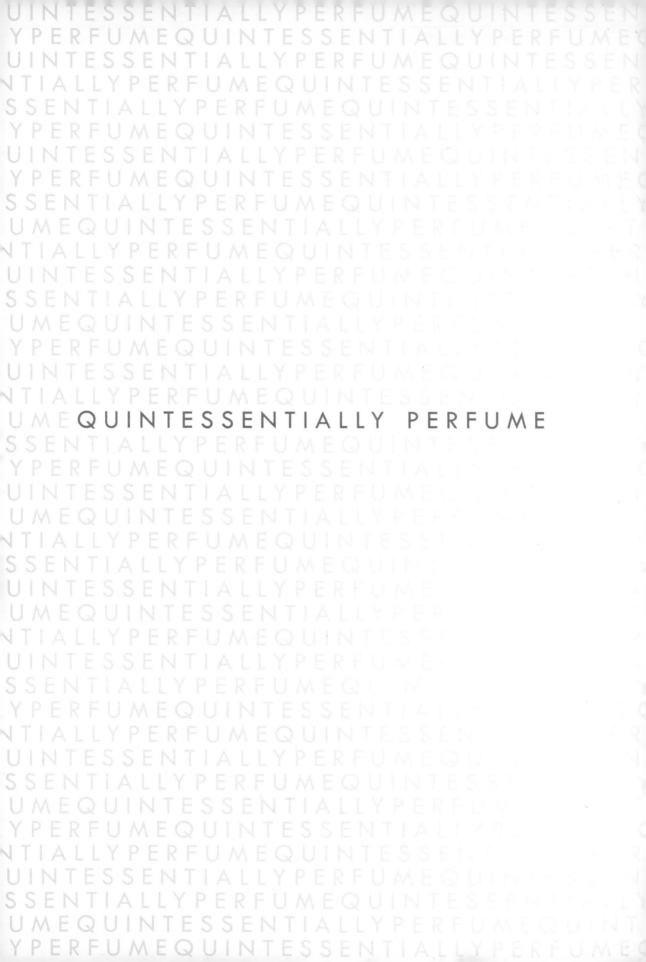

QUINTESSENTIALLY PERFUME

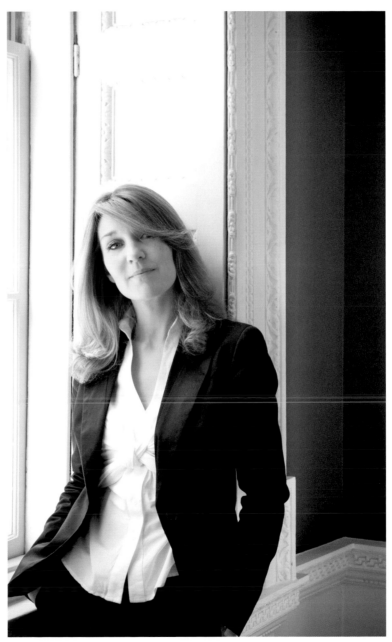

NATHALIE GRAINGER

I'm very proud to introduce you to Quintessentially Publishing's first fragrance title, Quintessentially Perfume. This book will take you on a journey of discovery revealing the stories, details and inspiration behind a selection of world class perfumers, their brands and the creations they offer us.

My fascination with perfume started very young and quickly evolved into a full blown and life-long love affair. I have been fortunate to work with a wide variety of perfumers and creators over the last decade and to gain understanding and knowledge that has inspired me in my consulting work and the creation of this book.

Quintessentially Publishing's dedication to luxurious services and products continues today with the perfume brands and houses featured within these pages. Quintessentially Perfume presents a rich and varied cross section of collections that cover different styles and approaches; brands whose appeal has gained mainstream recognition, as well as those who have deliberately sought to retain their niche identity. They hail from all corners of the world: France – whose southern town of Grasse has long been considered the world capital of perfume – Italy, Germany, Switzerland, The Netherlands, Austria, the United States and of course the UK, which boasts some of the world's most respected and influential perfume creators.

These featured perfume brands share an exceptional quality and beauty in their fragrances; a sense of innovation, a desire to honour the most precious raw materials and a ceaseless quest to captivate their followers at all times. Their works are inspired by emotions and tell moving, heartfelt stories. These pages showcase and applaud their merits and achievements; highlight their enduring relevance and reveal the role they play in the future of the perfume business.

In an age when instant response is the order of the day; when technology is omnipresent and we have witnessed the demise of face to face interaction, it seems vital to re-introduce some fundamentally human feeling into our everyday lives. Since the beginning of time our sense of smell has been key to our existence – warning us of danger and leading us to food. In the past perfume has been used to hide less pleasant smells by evoking thoughts of freshness and cleanliness. But fragrance also has the ability to play with our emotions, to stir up thoughts of love and romance, to revive distant memories and significant moments. It seems apt to cherish this sense which has direct access to what makes us special: our heart and our brain. And who better to turn to than the world's renowned experts and creators documented right here? I hope you enjoy this celebration as much as I have.

Introduction

Photo by Paul Raeside

5

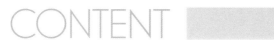

CONTENT

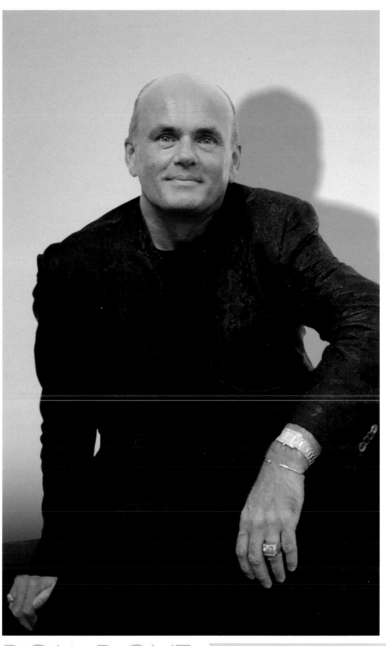

ROJA DOVE

Fragrance is the perfect example of the whole being greater than the sum of the parts. Hopefully this book will create a chink in a door that encourages you to step further in to explore the breadth of its creativity, the groundbreaking scents, the beauty of the bottles, the incredible artwork, the erudite penmanship, the raw materials, the places where the materials are sourced. Each aspect of perfumery is vast; each hope and dream huge.

I was utterly delighted when Quintessentially asked me to be Creative Advisor for this book. We drew up a list of some of the houses which represent the diversity of perfumery, and in their own ways have shaped the olfactory universe. We gathered together journalists who have distinctive voices, a point of view and a thorough understanding of what makes us, the brand and a scent tick. The result is a fantastic, eclectic melting pot of modern perfumery. Each of the houses represented has a very specific story to tell; the one constant – passion.

We wanted to create a book which looked at perfumery from different perspectives – that of the perfumer, the house, the owner, and the journalist. We wanted to create a book which looked at the old and the new, the large and the small. In doing so we hoped to create a book like no other; that is as eclectic as the industry itself.

As the great perfumer Edmond Roudnitska said, "The more we penetrate odours, the more they end up possessing us. They live within us and become an integral part of us...."

We hope you like the book we have created.

Roja Dove – Perfumer

123
456
789

PERFUME
THROUGH THE YEARS

PASSIONATE PERFECTION

Classic: Definition - Having lasting significance or worth; enduring.

There are two things which fundamentally determine whether a scent is likely to endure – quality of creativity and quality of materials.

Many people presume synthetics are somehow inferior and cheap. This is wrong. They can be. In the same way natural materials can be too. Natural jasmine can cost as little as £150 per kilo whereas the finest comes from the town of Grasse in the south of France and costs over £30,000 per kilo. It requires more than five million flowers picked at dawn before the sun touches them to obtain the precious oil. This pales into insignificance when you look at orris, the dried rhizome of the iris plant, which takes six years to process and costs some three and a half times the price of gold. A naturally occurring synthetic in the form of an isolate within is called orrisone and costs an additional 50%. Whereas natural ambergris comes in at a whopping ten times the price of gold. With each new creation a blend of natural materials are sublimate with newly discovered synthetics. They give the perfumer new possibilities, often costing fortunes to develop and produce, before being offered to the very best to work with. If the perfumer lives up to expectation a new scent will be created which will redefine perfumery and set a new trend. Others will try to follow the style but unless they use equally fine ingredients what they produce will be mediocre by comparison. So with the finest materials to hand the perfumer then has to set about the creative process.

Close your eyes and try to imagine a colour you have never seen before; if that is too difficult, try to imagine a sound you have never heard before; or, for the would be perfumer in you, try to imagine a smell you have never smelt before. Difficult isn't it? But that is exactly what a great perfumer has to do when working on a truly new creation. Drawing on a palette of thousands of materials they have to discern, divide, and harness a myriad of ingredients – a process which will often take many years. Without question this is one of the aspects that makes the story of scent such a fascinating and ever changing one.

The great classic fragrances have broken moulds, set trends and re-written the rules. Importantly they endure. They give rise to variations and imitations, but as in many fields, it is the originals that discerning people seek out while the imitators fall slowly by the wayside. Since commercial perfumery began at the very end of the 19th century, an average of 250 fragrances have been launched globally each year, which equates to some 30,000 fragrances in total. Of these less than 0.2% have achieved the status of being classed a true classic. In most instances it is the discovery of a new synthetic material which allows the perfumer to create an original harmony; sometimes due to an accident – an inadvertent overdose. As these new raw materials are developed, the perfumer will use their skill to harness the odours and hopefully shape a brand new olfactory signature. This can often take many years, in the case of the petrochemical derivatives known as aldehydes, nearly a quarter of a century. This indeed is the story of Chanel No5.

In 1903 many perfumers were trying to harness the newly discovered family of aldehydes, but it was Ernest Beaux who in 1921 with the creation of Chanel No5 defined a radically new floral style. He presented Gabrielle Chanel a selection of ten fragrances, each of which contained the very finest raw materials, each of them containing differing amounts of aldehydes. She chose the fifth trial, the bottle marked No5, where he had overdosed the aldehyde creating a shimmering new style unlike anything before. It was as radically modern as both Chanel and her views, and has become the most famous perfume in the world. As for its name, she was wildly superstitious and five was her lucky number. She also considered most fragrance names of the time 'sickly' and 'sappy' in their overt romanticism – this was as modern as Chanel herself.

Six years later in 1927 André Fraysse, who had also been working on the aldehydic theme, went off in a totally different direction. Using the effervescent olfactory effect of the aldehyde to make the ingredients cascade, he created another interpretation which was to become Lanvin's great classic Arpège. Here the aldehyde is buried deeply within the structure where it works alongside some 60 other ingredients; it is the conductor which releases the notes at just the right moment creating a perfectly harmonious arpeggio. The subtlety of this magnificent creation has allowed many variants and so makes it one of the most influential fragrances ever to have been produced. But none will compare – Jeanne Lanvin was adamant no material was too good for this scent which she gave to her daughter as a gift (as can be seen on the Paul Iribe leitmotif on the bottle).

Even as the world descended into the gloom of the Great Depression, Jean Patou was driven by his quest for ultimate luxury. "Wonderful," exclaimed Jean Patou, "this is it." He was smelling what was to become Joy. The perfumer Henri Alméras said, "You cannot use it commercially." "Why not?" Patou demanded. "It's too expensive, the price is too prohibitive," answered Alméras. "Nonsense," Patou said, "and I have got the perfect name for it, Joy. Wherever perfume is sold, Joy will be the standard of excellence; like Rolls Royce is to cars." Never had a scent used such enormous quantities of such high grade, high cost, high concentration, natural raw materials, and to this day its formula is untouched. The finest jasmine mingles with the other legendary note from Grasse: rose de Mai, which requires over 300,000 blooms to

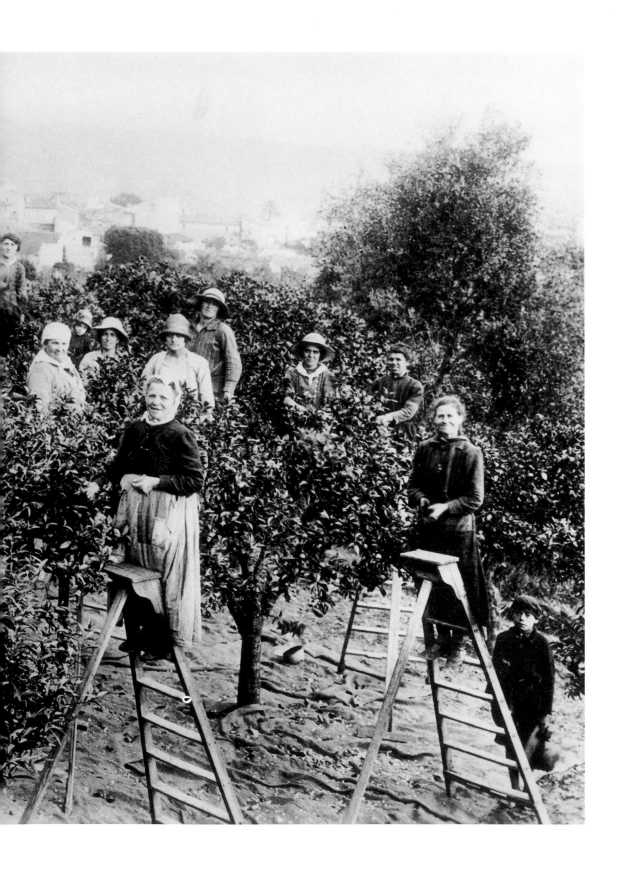

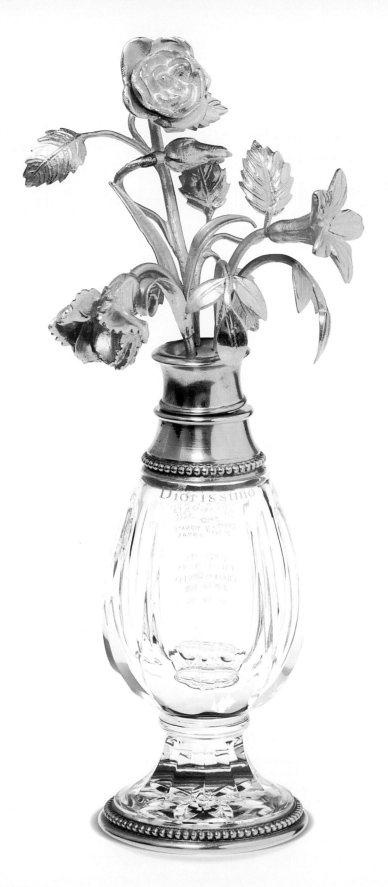

Diorissimo

create a kilo of oil. Joy is an unusual fragrance in that it uses the same notes to amplify and sublimate its luxurious central theme and in doing so it has fulfilled Patou's dream.

By 1948 the mood had shifted and Nina Ricci's L'Air du Temps perfectly captured the air of the times. This elegant creation fulfilled Nina Ricci's son Robert's belief about perfume; that perfume is not merchandise, but rather "its creation is an act of love." This beautiful scent was made even more desirable by the iconic Lalique flacon which houses it: two doves flying free which, when a woman caresses herself with them, as she applies fragrance, is reminded of the beautiful gentleness of this revolutionary scent. L'Air du Temps must be regarded as one of the most important perfumes ever to have been created. Launched after the turmoil of the Second World War, it is a masterpiece of simplicity. But its simplicity gives it its complexity, as it relies so heavily on fine quality natural raw materials which imbue it with a myriad of different olfactory facets. This effect shows the genius of its creator, Francis Fabron, who used a newly discovered material to amplify the warm spicy note of carnation in L'Air du Temps' heart.

Christian Dior's Diorissimo created by Edmond Roudnitska in 1956 is one of the only single floral creations to have survived. Why? To simplify is one thing, to stylise is something totally different. What Roudnitska managed to conjure up in this remarkable example of creativity is the freshness of nature reborn in spring. He was determined to pare down the formula, to move away from the big production numbers of many other fragrances of this time, to create something fresh and new. The result is in fact very complex, recreating the image of woodland: the floor alive with spring's new mantle and at its heart a delicate elusive blossom, a symbol of love, a highly stylised lily of the valley. A flower he believed would bring his creations luck and one which ultimately covered his coffin; the blooms spilling to the ground exuding their gentle, inimitable sweetness. This is Dior's Diorissimo.

By the mid 1960s men were beginning to place more importance on scent. Christian Dior's Eau Sauvage, created in 1966, is in my opinion one of the most important creations of the second half of last century. Created, like Diorissimo, by Edmond Roudnitska, it was the first fragrance to contain the newly discovered Hedione, or Di-hydro Jasmonate. This is a perfumer's dream material. It is one of the 900 or so molecular components found in jasmine and when isolated it has a pronounced citrus odour. It is far less volatile than a true citrus note and therefore has the advantage of lasting. Its slight floral aspect makes it an ideal 'connector', taking our nose smoothly from the fresh, citrus top notes to the sweeter more floral harmonies found in the heart. With its new, costly, lasting freshness, Eau Sauvage transformed both the chypré accord – in which woody, mossy notes are counter-pointed with brisk, fresh citrus notes – and the entire concept of masculine and feminine perfumery.

Some 20 years after Diorissimo, in 1977, the world was addicted to perfumer Jean-Louis Sieuzac's creation for Yves Saint Laurent – Opium. Sieuzac pushed the oriental notes of vanilla, resins and coumarin in a totally new direction; the small amounts it contains (only around 10%) give it enormous volume and presence suggesting a concentration some five times greater. These harmonies are given lift for the first time in the oriental accord by the inclusion of aldehydes around a central theme of rose and carnation. It was the first French fragrance to raise the concentration of 'juice' to unprecedented levels and the resulting, almost narcotic effect, was to fundamentally change the way future fragrances would be created. Also inspired by the orient was Jean-Jacques Diener's creation of 1981, which was surprisingly Cartier's first fragrance; they had designed a bottle in 1939 for a fragrance project but the war put a stop to it. What they eventually created was a contemporary oriental – Must de Cartier. Seventy years had passed since the first orientals were produced and, although most of the structure of the classic oriental accord remains intact; Cartier used many new raw materials ingeniously grafted onto the rich soft base,

imbuing Must de Cartier's oriental facet with a crisp freshness which had never been smelt before. Using their reputation as a luxury French jeweller as a starting point, their fragrance reflected their heritage, combining opulence with refinement; using only the world's finest raw materials they redefined the oriental accord.

Davidoff's Cool Water, created in 1988, was a further revolution in masculine perfumery. With its Adonis-like naked male imagery and its use of a dynamically fresh new wonder molecule, it became one of the most influential and successful masculine fragrances of all time and quickly became the blueprint for many imitations and still is to this day.

In 1992 Thierry Mugler launched his first fragrance, Angel. Created by Olivier Cresp and Yves de Chiris, this unprecedented scent shook the world and really did push fragrance in a whole new direction. Its secret is the paradoxical use of sugary sweet edible notes like candyfloss and toffee apples on a deep, earthy, ultra complex base around patchouli – which itself has an almost bitter chocolate note to it. The gum resins often associated with the oriental accord have been removed and the result has become the classical reference for a whole generation of oriental style fragrances. It was launched almost as a whisper campaign, each woman who smelt it fell under its spell, casting aside more traditional styles of oriental fragrances which, in comparison, seemed thick, old-fashioned and somewhat bourgeois. Both the fragrance and the bottle were almost impossible to perfect and it is only through the belief and determination of the former president of Parfums Thierry Mugler, Vera Strübi, that Angel became a stellar success – a modern classic.

Go back 100 years, when the perfumer was making for a few select clients, and the cost of raw materials did not matter as the clients were rich and demanded the finest, most costly ingredients. Today the modern world rarely allows perfumers carte blanche to use these rare materials when creating a new fragrance. Ironically exceptions come in the form of some of the oldest fragrance houses who are enjoying revivals in the quest for legitimacy and authenticity. This is true for Lubin with its great creations like Nuit de Longchamp; Grossmith, who revived three of their legendary scents not once taking into account the cost of the formulae; and most importantly of all Houbigant, who revived one of the most important scents of all time, Quelques Fleurs, whose influence can be found in nearly every other scent's structure. It is the scent which defined the floral bouquet with its blend of muguet, rose, jasmine, vanilla, sandalwood, and orris. We can see its influence on creations such as Chanel No5, Arpège, L'Air du Temps, and Madame Rochas – classics in their own right – alongside much more recent creations like the Tom Ford Musks. Also Houbigant's Fougère Royale – which was so influential it paved the way for modern perfumery through the inclusion of the first synthetic materials – had languished for years; I have had the pleasure of working on its recreation and not once until the formula was complete was I asked the cost. More recent additions would be Clive Christian, with the scents that bear his name. He sums it up eloquently thus: "In luxury and creativity there is a heartbeat that the financially driven just do not get."

Today marketing teams tend to work on research briefs, market analysis and minimising risk factors, resulting in fragrances that tend to be safe, similar and somewhat uniform. Luckily there are still people who believe vehemently and passionately in an olfactory project, and however many times they are told they should modify their creation, they believe enough in what they imagined when they closed their eyes and dreamt of a smell they had never smelt before, that another classic will slowly emerge and see the light of day. We will all be touched by it, and perfumery will once again go spiralling off in a new direction and these new illustrious fragrances will join the elite band of true classics.

Classic: Definition -A work recognised as definitive

Roja Dove

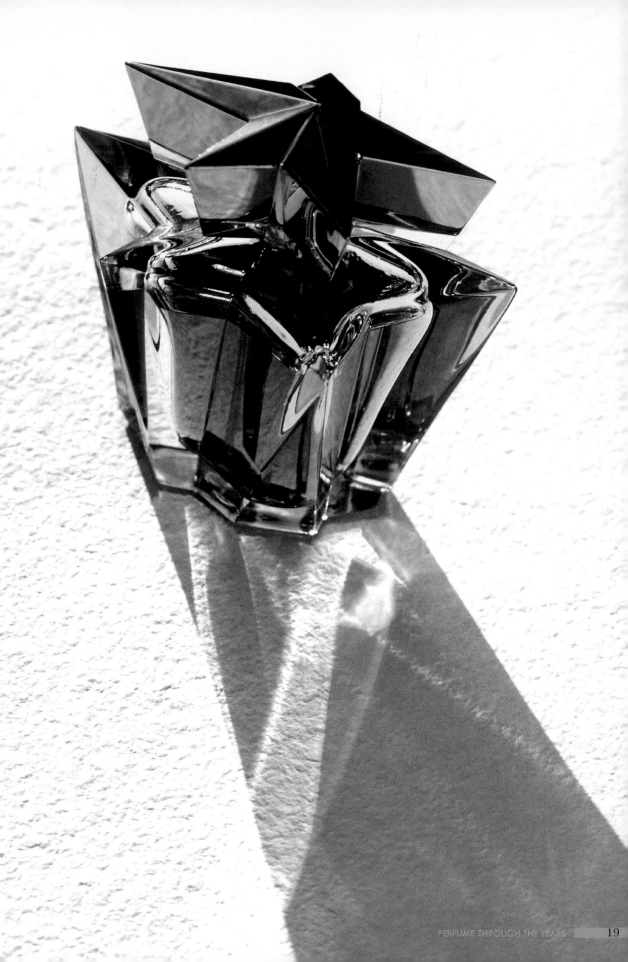

123
456
789

PERFUME INSPIRATION

STORIES THAT INSPIRE
BEAUTIFUL FRAGRANCES

The world's most enduring perfumes are inspired by some of the most beautiful and passionate love stories ever told: sweet narratives that reverberate in our hearts and minds long after any pleasure on the skin has dissipated. They conjure up images of sensuality and old-fashioned romanticism like nothing else can; holding us close, ensnared, spellbound.

Think of Guerlain's Shalimar. Sanskrit for 'temple of love', it is the name of the 17th century Emperor Shah Jehan's favourite Mughal gardens in Lahore where he would often walk with his beloved wife Mumtaz Mahal. The story goes that, lovesick and aggrieved after his wife's sudden death in childbirth, he touchingly dedicated his life to the creation of the Taj Mahal in honour of her memory. Likewise, the free-spirited Jicky was created by Aimé Guerlain and named after his sweetheart Jacqueline whom he wanted to marry (his nickname for her was Jicky), but it was never to be. Or L'Heure Bleue, the last great scent to be created before the First World War, it is said that Jacques found inspiration as he walked along the banks of the Seine at that fleeting, fragile moment in time (neither day nor night) when twilight falls. He encapsulated it forever in one of the most romantic perfumes ever created – the one his wife Lily always chose to wear.

Surely few can fail to be moved by the dramatic bouquet in Creed's Fleurissimo, created for Grace Kelly on her wedding day on behalf of her Prince Rainier; or the impending sadness in Caron's N'aimez Que Moi, which became a symbolic gift to wives and fiancées as French soldiers departed for the trenches; or even the more fiery Fracas, by Piguet, inspired by the single image of Hollywood legend Rita Hayworth in Gilda the epitome of femininity and eroticism, the 'Love Goddess', as she tosses back her mane of red hair. Others merely allude to the soft feminine form: Villoresi's Teint de Neige, a soft powdery scent that sketches a picture of

a delicate young girl sitting at a lacy glass dressing table, powdering her face and illuminating her exquisite skin; or Frederic Malle's En Passant, the image of a young girl on a warm green morning in early spring, strolling along the banks of the Seine, catching wafts of fresh white lilac buds over a wall.

Perfume has a unique ability to capture our bitter sweet, cherished memories, to hold them dear and revive treasured thoughts with startling clarity and emotion at any given moment with one sharp intake of breath. For, unlike our other senses, smell channels fragrance directly to the brain's limbic system: the emotional part of the brain, home to our memory and imagination. So when you detect a fragrance you haven't experienced for a long time – perhaps that scent you wore on your own wedding day, or your first date – you can picture every detail: from the rustle of the gown, the sound of laughter and music, each warm embrace, the rush of unexpected happiness. Or indeed, you may quiver with a deep sadness should that memory be of some heartfelt loss. Much like hearing a piece of music that can instantly take you back to a certain time and place, the faintest trace of a fragrance can evoke strong memories and powerful reactions from within. And every one of us has our own olfactory memory which is completely individual and made up of all our personal experiences. A single drop of perfume has the ability to revive the dream and memory of loved ones past and present.

We relate to perfume perfectly. Imagination stirs the senses. And when a love of something or someone is the inspiration behind the drive to create a fragrance, the story of this passion intrigues us, captures our heart, ensnares it, echoes our moods and emotions and, according to leading perfumers, makes us feel closer to either the creator or the muse. This may inspire us in some way, sparking us to buy a fragrance and ultimately to wear it.

"What inspires me the most in the world is... women," says Francois Demarchy, Director of Olfactory Development for LVMH. "For me, composing a perfume is much easier when I have the image of a woman in my head. I think this is important to the women that wear my fragrances because they know that they were a part of the creative process." Likewise Jean-Paul Guerlain recalls, "My grandfather (Jacques Guerlain) used to say that a successful fragrance is one whose scent exactly matches the dream or vision that inspired it. It is the story of a

ROBERT
PIGUET
PARIS-FRANCE

fracas
DE
ROBERT
PIGUET
PARIS - FRANCE

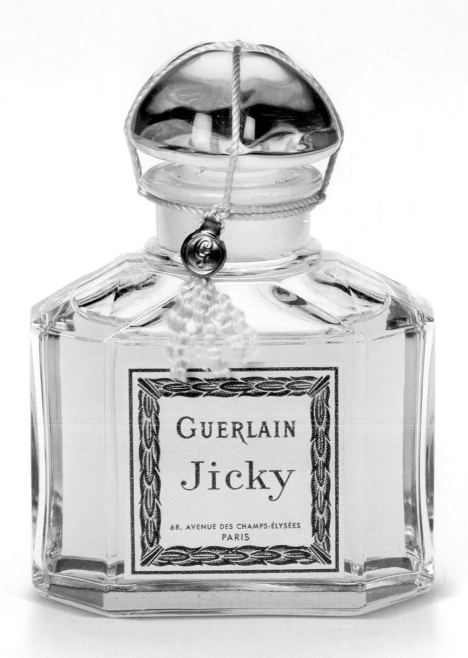

sublime and sensual passion. My point of departure in the quest of this sensuality may be a smile, the fragrance of a woman's skin, the fleeting vision of a face. Every one of our fragrances was inspired by a muse. Behind each one, you find yourself in the presence of a woman who was loved or admired." So we put ourselves in her shoes...

"Most consumers are looking for a sensory experience and to live a dream," says Françoise Donche, nose for Parfums Givenchy. "To bring a story is a way to strengthen the relationship between a product and her users, to give them culture, and interest, to allow them to dream, and above all to seduce. In a world where speed and stress are permanent, stories are very necessary and provide highly pleasant moments. They act like an 'oasis'. They bring refreshment, reflexion and enrich the mind." "When a fragrance has a story behind it, it makes it more real, more alive, more true" adds Lyn Harris. "It has more emotion, something more to connect with. It's always easier to relate to something like this, with a story, with nostalgia, rather than something abstract."

Of course, the moment we fall under the spell of a scent, stories no longer exist in the realm of fancy, or in the dreams and imaginings of a perfumer. The storys swiftly become our own, as too does the perfume. So forget the bottle, the packaging, the dreams sold therein, it is our own unique association thereafter that makes a perfume irreplaceable in our lives: the memories of an instance, a perfect picture that never fades, encapsulated like a molecular moment of magic, fleeting, imperceptible, elusive. A perfume is loved because of a single slice of our own life, our own love story, be it partner, lover, father, mother or child.

Like a secret haunting of the senses, fragrance touches our nerve centre and knows no boundaries. It touches and becomes an integral part of us for eternity. For me, that one swift intake of Le Dix or Je Reviens – both my late mother's life-loved scents – releases a raw intensity of emotion and I am swiftly moved to tears. The stories are now of my own making; my memories of every cherished hug and kiss, that most heavenly bond that really does rip the heart and soul apart once it is gone, are placed upon a pedestal, to be loved and revered for eternity. Much like a favourite story... much like a well-loved scent. Too touching for words.

Jo Glanville-Blackburn

123
456
789

PERFUME BOTTLES

HOME OF DREAMS

As I open the bottle, the liquid escapes like a genie transporting me in an instant to my childhood, my first sexual encounter, my lover's arms, or home. As a very small child I remember stealing into my mother's bedroom and opening the bottles of scent on her dressing table amazed by their beautiful, glamorous shapes, and the enormous breadth of odours which emanated from them. As Gabrielle Chanel said about her own empty scent bottles, "the bottles are my memories of surrender and conquest – my crown jewels of love." Often the bottle is the last link with the past – the physical proof of scents lost.

Beautiful flacons have existed since antiquity, but it was the industrial revolution that enabled the development of commercial bottles and brought about the abundance of pieces that form the basis of most of the world's important collections. Two houses, more than any others, changed the way scent was presented forever – Baccarat and Lalique. Baccarat with its peerless reputation created impeccable, classical designs throughout the 19th and the start of the 20th centuries. For anyone dealing in luxury, nothing else would do. So François Coty, like most fine perfumers, used Baccarat flacons. He was to change perfumery forever and in doing so earned the title, 'the father of modern perfumery'. He was the first to use the newly available bases which all the other perfumers were frightened of and, in doing so, created some of the most original accords ever smelt. He created a demand for newness and helped to forge the industry as we know it today. He came with what is now considered an industry staple: the idea of colour coding each fragrance so that his clients could easily identify 'their' scent. He asked his next-door-neighbour, René Lalique, if he would design a label for his bottles. He created a label in glass for Coty's scent L'Effleur, the label was applied to a very classical Baccarat bottle. Lalique expanded the idea and created a bottle around the label along with a box. And so conceptual packaging was born. Coty could not have imagined how far-reaching his actions would be, nor how enduring.

His earliest works were achieved using a process known as *cire-perdue* or lost-wax. The mould is made from wax which is much softer than metal and allows far greater intricacy of design. The problem is that the mould is destroyed by the heat of the molten glass making mass production impossible. Lalique, therefore, chose to work in a new type of glass he'd developed called demi-crystal, which had a very low lead content, as opposed to the crisp brightness of traditional crystal. The lead was necessary as it made the glass softer and less brittle, allowing him to employ a new semi-automated manufacturing process. This new material worked perfectly with the soft, often sinuous designs that typified his work and that of the Art Nouveau movement which he played a significant part in popularising. It allowed him to create a new type of bottle half mass produced and half the work of the artisan – it was a revolution.

Many other artists were important at this time; Louis Chalon created the flacon for Roger and Gallet's Bouquet Nouveau; Lucien Gaillard worked with Violet, an important house of the time; and Alphonse Mucha also designed bottles directly. But it is Julien Viard and André Jollivet who looked as though they might be Lalique's biggest rivals. Viard's most important creation to still be in production is Le Narcisse Noir which he created for Caron. When it was launched it was one of the most copied bottles of all time. He developed what are known today as figural stoppers, one of the most beautiful examples being Lubin's Magda with its gilded woman's face forming the stopper.

It was however the collaboration of François Coty and René Lalique that formed the catalyst which transformed the industry. It was perfectly in tune with the changes in society that had bought about the middle classes and an unprecedented demand for luxury and newness. The aforementioned L'Effleur altered bottle design forever. In 1908 Lalique created a bottle for Coty's Ambre Antique with a frieze of Athenian women heightened with a sepia patina. In 1909 he created a bottle for another Coty scent, Cyclamen. It was the first time the house name along with that of the scent and the glass artist appeared on the bottle as part of the design – everything was visible, everything was new. When combined with the new coloured patinations Lalique had also pioneered, labels seemed redundant and old fashioned. The demand for his work was enormous, he started to accept commissions from other perfume houses such as Piver, as well as creating bottles which he sold empty in his own store. The demand was so great he rented an old glass factory along with its staff. Twelve months later he was able to buy the factory outright.

He developed his distinctive style very quickly and by 1919 he had perfected what was to become one of his specialities – the tiara stopper. One of the most technically difficult is the Bouchon Fleurs de Pommier created for Volnay in 1919, which has a polished edge, piercing, and patination – it set the standard for the style. Aesthetically it was only surpassed by D'Orsay's Leurs Armes. By now he was creating for most of the great perfume houses such as Worth, Houbigant, Roger and Gallet, Guerlain, and Coty. Although Guerlain was the only house that asked Lalique not to sign their pieces as they felt they did not need another company's name to help them sell their own.

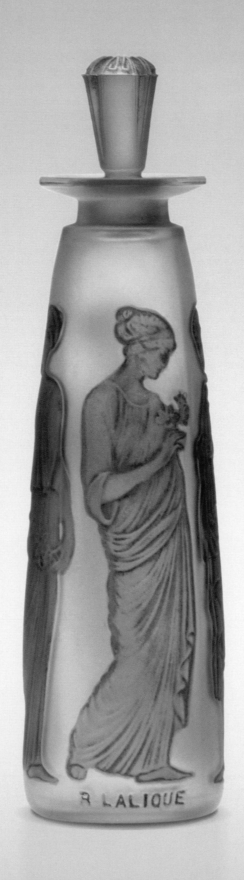

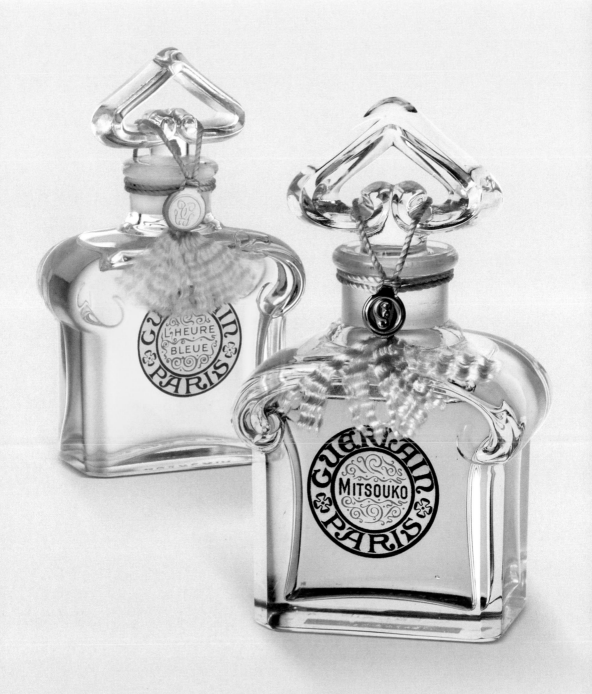

The 1920s saw some of the most ravishing of all his designs as well as some of the most modernist which he created for Molinard and Worth respectively. Molinard's Le Baiser du Faune was created in 1928 and features so many of the techniques Lalique perfected; in particular that of indenting the centre of the bottle thus creating a 'halo' around a central panel for the scent. In this piece the central panel depicts a faun kissing a young maiden – a recurring theme in the 1920s. Calendel was created in 1929 with a frieze of naked women surrounding the bottle – each of them gazing up toward the bouquet of flowers which make the stopper. Les Isles d'Or, of the same year, has a frieze of naked women around the upper part of its square form.

Worth's Sans Adieu looked like an extra from Fritz Lang's Metropolis with its 'electrical' stopper. Or the skyscraper inspired creation for Je Reviens looks like it has stolen its colour from the sky. These creations form part of a wonderful whole – five flacons to house five scents which tell one of the most beautiful stories our industry has ever created – the ultimate fragrant love-letter: Dans la Nuit, Vers le Jour, Sans Adieu, Je Reviens, Vers Toi – 'In The Night, Just Before Dawn, With no Goodbye, I Will Return, To You.'

Baccarat in contrast created the most diverse number of styles of flacons perfecting highly sophisticated techniques like double and triple casing. A rarely used process, in which one or two different colours of crystal have clear crystal blown into them. The crystal is then painstakingly cut away to reveal the brilliant, clear crystal within. Baccarat's masterstroke was to ignore the work of Lalique and to exploit their own great strengths – technical know-how and quality. There had never been a Mr. Baccarat so they were not constrained to a particular style. They employed a young man as head of their design studio who was to prove himself as one of the leading lights of the Art Deco movement: the sculptor George Chevalier. His ability to create an unendingly diverse number of designs appealed to the couturier who engaged him as well as all the leading perfume houses of the period. He designed many of the most famous bottles of the period, some of which are still in production today; like Guerlain's 1911 Gendarme design for the L'Heure Bleue and Mitsouko bottle, albeit they are no longer in Baccarat crystal. The demand for their work was so enormous that they were producing around 5,000 bottles per day.

As the Art Nouveau movement took hold Baccarat embraced it, as can be seen in three of their designs for D'Orsay: Meggy has three flowers on the stopper which perfectly reflect the top of the bottle; Toujours Fidèle with its rampant dog encapsulated two sub-themes – that of the figural stopper and that of animalism; and Leurs Armes whose body was made of four interlinked maidens. The First World War made it difficult. Everybody looked to reduce costs. None more so than Coty who decided to open his own glass factory and set about enlisting Baccarat's staff offering huge pay increases. Baccarat was furious and matched the offer, severing all business ties with him for almost 30 years. Not only did he upset Baccarat, he also enraged Lalique as he decided to continue using Lalique's designs without paying him a royalty. Whilst he left a trail of upset, his business continued to grow and was about to become the largest the industry has ever known.

Baccarat under Chevalier's stewardship continued to create highly influential designs, including many for the Decorative Arts Fair of 1925 (which gave us the term Art Deco); one of the most perfect being that for Gabilla's 1926 Mon Talisman. These designs played their part in the onset of modernism and cubism, some of the best examples of which were created for Houbigant, Silka, Ybry and Piver. The public's thirst for luxury, novelty, and modernity was relentless and was captured perfectly in one of the most decadent bottles ever made – Guerlain's iconic Papillon bottle for Coque d'Or (shell of gold). This bottle, inspired by the androgyny of the likes of Marlene Dietrich, comprised a bow tie made from cobalt crystal totally covered in a fine shell of pure gold leaving just the shoulders exposed to reveal the luxurious crystal within; the whole encased in a silk lined box created by Jean-Michel Frank.

Having re-enforced their position as the pre-eminent supplier of luxury bottles, their reputation continued to attract new clients after the Second World War; both Rochas and Dior commissioned bottles. Baccarat embraced surrealism and the whims of one of the most creative of all designers, Schiaparelli. Her great friend Dali designed a bottle which captured the spirit of the times perfectly for her scent Le Roi Soleil (the Sun King). It depicted the sun rising over the darkness of the world, with free-flying birds making the eyes, eyebrows, nose, lips, and cheeks, the whole making the stopper. The bottle itself made up of the ocean nestling in a duchesse silk lined shell case. Whereas her scent Shocking was held in a bottle in the shape of a woman's torso, a tape measure slung around its shoulders, and a bouquet of crystal flowers wrapped around its gilded stopper suggesting the scent emanating from the wearers neck. We still see the influence of the design today – it was this bottle which inspired Jean-Paul Gaultier's bottle for his scent Classique.

The great age of luxury bottle design was created in 1956 for Christian Dior's Diorissimo: a beautiful Baccarat amphora with gilded bronze fittings surmounted by a vase of flowers. Its beauty is encased in gold.

From time to time perfume houses still commission great new designs in crystal. That said, one of the most important was created by Baccarat themselves for the scent Les Larmes Sacrées de Thebes. Ironically this bottle calls to mind the pyramids where the world's first perfume formula for the scent Kypi was found. And so, when we open it and breath in its scent we are reminded of the ancient Egyptians' great belief that perfume has the ability to make us immortal. I don't know if that is really true, but one thing is for certain, these bottles contain the precious liquids that in a nano-second can transport us back to the most precious moments of our lives.

'With one breath of her scent I forfeit my kingdom, with another I forfeit my soul.'

Roja Dove

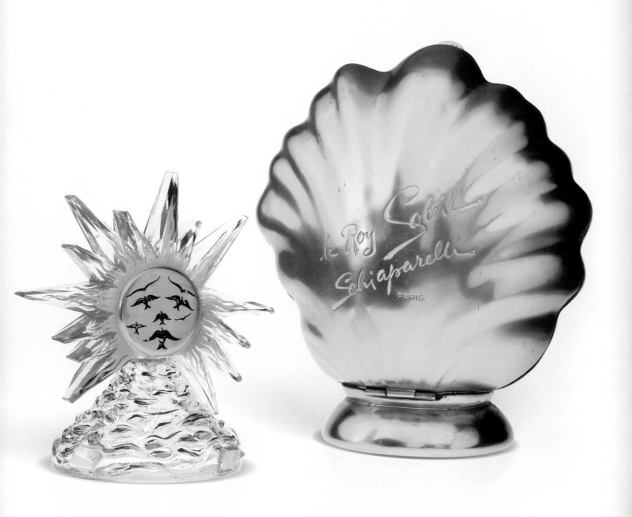

123
456
789

HUMAN
REACTION TO PERFUME

SENSUAL MEMORIES

'There's rosemary; that's for remembrance. Pray, love, remember.' Hamlet.

Poor Ophelia. She never got to carry fresh sprigs to her wedding and Shakespeare forgets to tell us whether Hamlet had the grace to lay them on her grave. What we do know is that for millennia the perfume of plants has marked our milestones, from cradle to coffin – archaeologists have discovered traces of flowers in tombs dating back to Neolithic times.

It's now believed that early man's sense of smell was keener than his vision – and could mean the difference between life and death. Scents enabled him to navigate his world and its imperatives, attractions and hazards. The first area of the human brain to develop was a primitive olfactory cortex which later grew into the amygdale, part of the limbic system which also houses touch, vision, taste and emotional centres. Memory too is processed here, which explains why an unexpected whiff of perfume can trigger a multi textured, instant recall – what you wore, who you loved, the music you played and the food you shared when you first wore that scent all come flooding back.

It has become virtually impossible to talk about scent memory without mentioning the French novelist Marcel Proust, whose 1913 epic *Remembrance of Things Past* hinges on the sweet, cakey scent of a madeleine dipped in tea, which provokes a tsunami of vivid childhood longings. Proust is the poster boy for 'déjà smell'; it's largely thanks to him that we have come to regard fragrance as the most potent of all sensual memory prompts. Yet according to American neuroscientist Dr. Avery Gilbert, scent-induced involuntary memory may not be as indelible as Proust would have us believe. In his *What the Nose Knows*, Gilbert argues that not only must scent memory be learned, it's also easily confused. Sniffing one scent after another simply means you forget what went before – and we've all been there in department stores. This, however, doesn't explain why it's almost impossible to 'enjoy', what your rational mind tells you, is a perfectly lovely scent because someone you can't stand wears it! So how reliable are scents as aide-memoires? There's a centuries old-Chinese tradition of passing round spice or incense when families gather to share their history. According to Dr. Rachel Herz, world-renowned scent psychologist and author of *The Scent of Desire* this is context dependent memory in practise. "Recreating the same environment or mindset as when you learned something aids your data retrieval mechanisms," she says. Central to the context is remembering how you feel when you're there. Studies have confirmed that if you scent the room where you study, sniff the same scent during a test or exam, it will prompt your memory. More power to that aromatherapy candle? "But," says Herz, "the smell has to be distinctive or unusual to work. Sniff a new scent for each topic you're trying to learn and don't confuse them," is her advice.

Which leads us to scent as cognitive therapy. Avery Gilbert has led a study that suggests you can consciously use your easy breezy, happy holiday fragrance to airlift you out of the doldrums back home. And don't fret when that 'for one summer only' limited edition expires; in a paper published in the (US) *Journal of Mental Imagery*, Gilbert claims that even imagining a scent can feel as real as actually sniffing it. "The very act of remembering a fragrance activates an entire range of psycho physical responses," he maintains. "The full quota of sensory impressions such as sounds, textures, colours and emotions cascade in," he adds. Virtual scent, anyone?

Of course, nothing hits the spot like the real thing. For years I have relied on patchouli as my personal security blanket, insulating me against diffidence and depression. Each time I inhale its earthy, subversive, treacly euphoria from the palms of my hands, I'm my schoolgirl self in Kensington Market at the end of the '60s, exhilarated by life's potential and the shock of the new.

Yes, scent memories are precious and subjective. They can also be collective, and cultural influences are key. In the west, vanilla's sweet baby powder and custard associations make it almost universally reassuring and, according to studies reported by the Smell and Taste Institute in Chicago, men especially find it an irresistible stimulant. According to fragrance expert, Roja Dove, this probably has less to do with nursery nostalgia than the fact that vanilla is a psychogenic aphrodisiac! Heliotropin – vanilla's main chemical – also has useful sedative effects. A study at the Sloan-Kettering hospital in New York has found that the 'homely' aroma helps patients undergoing MRI scans to feel less anxious and claustrophobic.

Actively exploiting a fragrance has to be the most sensual means of hitting a natural (and legal) high. As I'm writing this on a chill and dingy London afternoon, my mood is subtly manipulated by the scent of orange blossom – one of perfumery's surest blue-sky thinkers – emanating from the collection of summer editions on my desk. Distilled from the bitter orange (bigarade) tree, its breezy freshness and comforting spicy undertones qualify 'fleurs d'oranger' as the euphoric element in countless summery florals. It is a potent antidote to grey-day gloom. Bigarade's influence is legendary throughout the Mediterranean. Nervous brides carry posies of it, exhausted mothers bribe children with cakes flavoured with its floral water (that soggy madeleine again!) and perfumers use it to conjure the lazy, sexy warmth of sun (or suntan lotion) on skin. Currently enjoying a lively revival (dispersing post recession angst, perhaps?) orange blossom has also enjoyed a long standing, starring role in Houbigant's Quelques Fleurs and Guerlain's L'Heure Bleue, both hauntingly beautiful floral fragrances from 1912. To celebrate its UK comeback last year, I presented my 98 year old mother with a bottle of Quelques Fleurs – the youthful favourite she still wore throughout my childhood. Her eyes welled instantly. "Oh those dances…" she mused. And here's a curious thing; until recently I've never consciously made the connection between these two grand old matriarchs of the floral family, yet the bitter sweet and elusively smoky L'Heure Bleue has always filled me with an unaccountably tearful longing. Could it be that this exquisite fragrance also reminds me of my mother?

Vicci Bentley

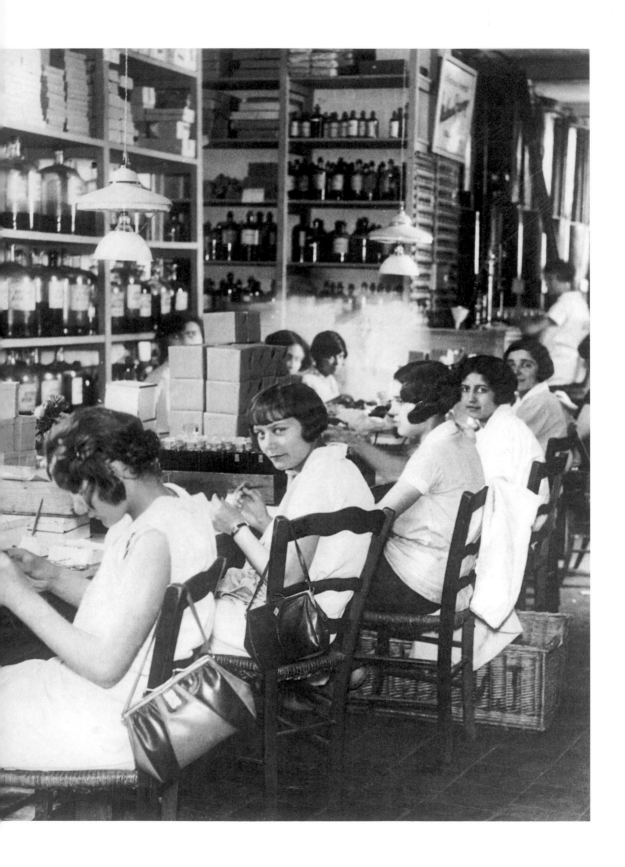

SCENT AND GENDER

Are you man enough to wear Chanel No5? Or woman enough to splash on Azzaro Pour Homme? I have to admit that I've never been a great fan of cross-dressing, but what I'd like to do in this chapter is to persuade you that to distinguish between 'masculine' and 'feminine' fragrances makes about as much sense as 'male' or 'female' art, music or food, for that matter. The fact that we divide perfumes into men's or women's fragrances has less to do with logic than it has to do with marketing, packaging and conventional thinking – and if you look back it's not even that old a distinction.

Once upon a time perfumes were perfumes, and there appears to have been little in terms of a gender divide until the early 20th century. Men wore fragrances which today we'd almost certainly regard as outrageously effete: both Napoleon and Wagner were famous for drenching themselves in scent and Victorian gentlemen favoured sweetly scented floral perfumes alongside the ubiquitous eau de Cologne. Even the words themselves – fragrance, perfume, scent – are genderless; the daft male-only term 'aftershave' appears only to have been dreamed up in the 1920s as a marketing wheeze. The expression may have made perfume sound a bit more butch and manly, all too often (in the days before male moisturiser became acceptable) it also left the more literal-minded chap with a burning face and peeling skin.

But surely there are some obvious differences between men's and women's fragrances? Of course there are, and I'm not suggesting that male readers should rush out and purchase the olfactory equivalent of a pair of pink frilly knickers. Some scents (naming no names) are so insanely sweet and girly that it would be hard for even the most rugged male to get away with wearing them. But then, these also tend to be the kinds of perfume that, to be frank, smell as ludicrous on a grown woman as they would on any self respecting man.

Beyond these parodies of perfume, there are remarkably few fragrances that, if you trust your nose and can brace yourself to ignore everything you've been told by breathless adverts and terrifyingly made-up sales assistants, are as incontrovertibly feminine or masculine as to be completely unwearable by either sex. But one famous example is Christian Dior's Eau Sauvage. Launched in 1966, it quickly established itself as a hugely popular men's fragrance and has stayed on the best seller lists ever since. I think most men would agree that there are few more bracing, fresh and (above all) masculine fragrances around. I couldn't agree more, but if you're a fan of Eau Sauvage, next time you're in a well-stocked perfume store, wander over to the women's perfume counter and have a smell of Diorella, launched just six years later and designed by the same perfumer, the legendary Edmond Roudnitska. The first time I smelled it I thought, "But this is Eau Sauvage!" And it is, give or take some extra fruitiness which, you could say, gives it a slightly more girly character – though perfume guru Luca Turin regards it as a perfected Eau Sauvage and one of the best masculines money can buy.

In many ways it's easier this way around, women seem always to have been less inhibited about adopting fragrances that were originally intended for the opposite sex. Eau Sauvage is a classic example; whether they smelled it on their boyfriends or discovered it for themselves, women quickly recognised it as the masterpiece it is and those in the know have been wearing it ever since. Guerlain's superb Vetiver is, to my mind, one of the most archetypically masculine perfumes in existence, yet it too has long been a female favourite – the olfactory equivalent of an Yves Saint Laurent tuxedo.

More striking still are those fragrances that have crossed the gender divide more or less entirely. When Aimé Guerlain launched Jicky in 1889 it was initially bought by men; at the time its sharp, slightly catty smell was considered too overtly sexual in character for respectable women to risk wearing. By the 1920s though, liberated by the rise of female emancipation, women started using Jicky too, and gradually it became a 'female' fragrance – although a few self-confident men (Sean Connery being the most often cited example) continue to wear it today. Chanel's super plush Cuir de Russie followed a similar trajectory, although it would be hard, even now, to define it as either masculine or feminine in character.

Visit a standard issue perfume store and you'd be forgiven for thinking that we were still living in a world where men were men and women were women and never the twain should meet; as if history had got stuck around 1955 and all the social and sexual revolutions since then had never actually happened. But society, of course, has changed and there are encouraging signs that, at least parts, of the perfume industry have begun to realise that dividing fragrance along crude gender lines is weirdly outdated. A handful of future-looking perfume brands such as Byredo, Comme des Garçons and Escentric Molecules, already offer 'genderless' fragrances. And there is a growing trend for imaginative retailers to follow their lead, stocking perfumes by brand instead of dividing them into men's and women's scents.

Perfume customers are changing too. While the majority of people may continue (for the moment at least) to accept the status quo, a small but growing band of perfume lovers are happy to think for themselves, without choosing perfume on the basis of its supposed masculinity or femininity. The trick is simply to follow your nose; to choose the perfumes you love, like the people you love, regardless of what other people might say.

Christopher Stocks

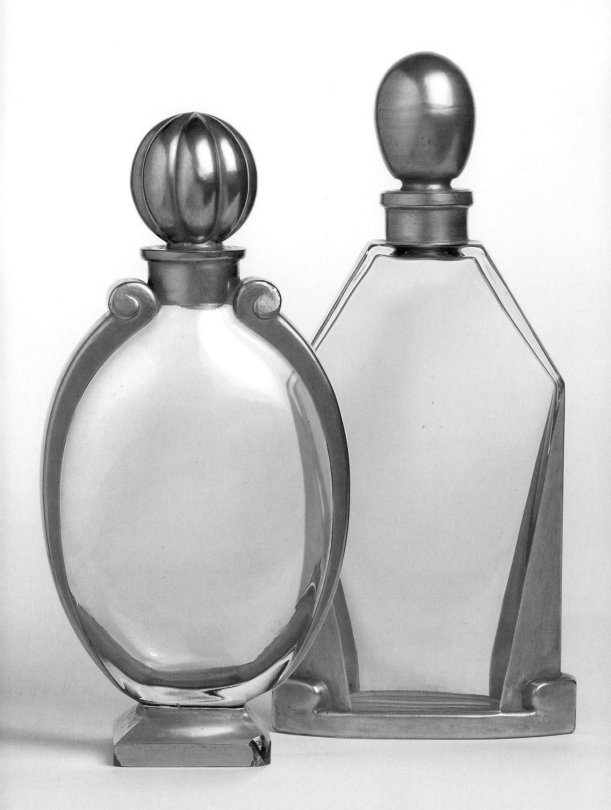

123
456
789

THE LANGUAGE
OF PERFUME

1925 Caron. L'Infini

1957 Dior. Diorling

1925 Jean Patou. Amour Amour

1914 Guerlain. Parfum des Champs Elysées

1917 Ramsès Le secret du Sphinx

1929 Gabilla, La vierge folle

1921 Lubin, Kismet

1925 Caron, Nuit de Noel

1900 Royal Vaissier

Absolute
Absolutes are the purest form of essential oil and as a result are extremely costly. They are obtained through a process where the oil is removed by a solvent resulting in a thick waxy paste known as a concrete. The concrete contains odourless waxes known as stearoptene's which need to be removed from the concrete by washing it with alcohol. The alcohol is then removed by evaporation under reduced pressure to avoid damaging the resulting oil.

Accord
Accords are blends of two or more materials that produce a new effect that is different to the individual parts. Certain classical accords are the mainstay of perfumery. Great creations however are produced by perfumers creating new and highly original accords.

Agrumen (or Hesperidic or Citrus)
Agrumens are more commonly referred to as citrus oils.The correct perfumery term for these oils is hesperidic or hesperides. See also 'citrus' and 'hesperidic'.

Aldehyde
Aldehydes are highly aromatic chemicals that naturally occur in many plants but are generally obtained from alcohol and the refraction of petroleum. They were discovered towards the end of the 19th century although there is much debate as to exactly when and who by. They are used in the manufacture of scented synthetic materials but the most famous are the ones prefixed with the letter C such as C12 and C12mna. These add the sparkling effect in classical aldehydic creations such as Chanel No5 and Arpège. Generally all aldehydes from C12 down add a sparkling effect, whereas all aldehydes from C14 up offer a fruity effect as illustrated in Guerlain's Mitsouko with its peachy C14 note.

Amber
Amber causes more confusion than any other term in the perfumery world. Used correctly it was always an abbreviation for ambergris and should be used to describe the synthetic ones. Over time the word has been used to describe the soft, balsamic qualities which exude from ambergris but are also found in other materials – labdanum being the best example, along with tolu and Peru balsams. Labdanum produces a costly extract called ambrein which is highly reminiscent of ambergris. The greatest confusion however comes from the use of the term to describe Oriental perfumes in French which are often referred to as ambrée.

Ambergris
Ambergris is the legendary and valuable ingredient that is found floating in the sea or cast upon the shore. It is a substance that is excreted by the sperm whale after it has been feeding on cuttlefish. See also 'amber'.

Animal Note (or Animalic)
Animal notes add an incomparable sensuality and lasting quality to a creation. Today most of the animal notes are recreated synthetically for ecological and moral reasons. The Swiss firm of Firmenich won the Nobel Prize back in the early part of last century for their work synthesizing them. The most famous which come, or came, directly from animals are, ambergris, castoreum, civet, musk, and beeswax. Some plant materials also yield oils that are animalic such as birch and labdanum which offer a Leather Note to a creation. See also 'leather notes'.

Aoud
Aoud is deep and intense oil crafted from fragrant resin harvested from the heart of the aquilaria tree. Richly complex and warm, the scent intensifies as the aoud matures.

Arabic Perfumery
Arabic perfumery has been active since the dawn of history, with many of the most legendary exotic ingredients being indigenous to the region. These include frankincense, myrrh, labdanum, taif rose and aoud.

Aromachology
Aromachology is the study of the psychological and fundamental effect odours have on our being; the University of Japan has championed much of this work.

Aromatherapy
Aromatherapy uses the scent of plants and flowers to increase our sense of wellbeing.

Aromatic
Aromatic means something scented or fragrant. In perfumery the correct use of this term is to describe the scent herbaceous ingredients such as sage, lavender, rosemary, basil, bay etc.. These materials generally make up the creations 'head notes'.

Atomiser
Atomiser refers to a container that is sealed and allows a liquid to be sprayed. The french term for this is vaporisateur. They were first designed as throat sprays because fragrance was applied from bottles – as it had been since antiquity.

Attar (or Otto)

Attar as a term is very old-fashioned and comes from the Arabic word for perfume, Itr. It refers to an essential oil, which is an oil produced by distillation. Distillation was perfected in Persia (now Iran) where a perfume is referred to as Atr.

Balsam (or Balm)

Balsams are sometimes referred to as balms and refer to thick resins that exude from the bark of certain trees and shrubs. They work as excellent fixatives and often have a soft, sometimes vanillic quality. Peru, tolu and storax (styrax) are some of the best known.

Balsamic

Balsamic is a term used to describe the soft qualities balsams impart to a fragrance.

Base Notes

The longest lasting of fragrance ingredients that form the foundation of the metaphorical fragrance triangle. Correctly split into two sections, the base and the deep base; the former consists of woods, mosses and spices, and the latter of fixatives and balsams.

Batteuse

Batteuse is a devise traditionally used to remove the oils from concretes using alcohol.

Benzoin

Benzoin is a sweet-smelling balsamic resin.

Bergamot

Bergamot is a citrus fruit about the size of an orange but with a yellow-green colouration akin to a lemon. Its odour is less bitter than the lemon.

Blotter (or Scent Strip or Mouillette)

A professional tool made from special paper that is used to apply fragrances for appraisal.

Chypré

Chypré is a term applied to a specific accord developed by François Coty in 1917 based around a blend of patchouli, gum resins, cedarwood, vetiver, rose and jasmine; counter-pointed by bergamot with a dominant note of oakmoss running throughout the structure. The term is French for Cypress and most likely originated as a name for a scent during the time of the Crusades although it is believed that it dates back to the time of the ancient Romans. Many houses lay claim to originating it, but without question it is the Coty creation which defines the modern Chypré. The Chypré is one of the main fragrance families.

Citrus (Agrumen or Hesperidic)

Citrus notes refer to the oils obtained from the rind of citrus fruits. They give a fresh, dynamic, citrus feel to a creation and are often used to counterpoint richer materials used later in a composition. They are also called hesperidic notes.

Comité Français du Parfum (CFP)

The Comité Français du Parfum was founded in 1966 to promote the supremacy of French perfumery. It lays down the standards generally adhered to by the industry. It is also responsible for inaugurating and maintaining the Osmothèque at Versailles, just outside Paris, which is a fragrance museum/library for perfumers. It enables them to discover and study many creations which have disappeared from the market yet still influence creations today.

Coumarin

Coumarin is found in many plants and fruits, but it is the tonka bean that perfumers use as it is rich in natural coumarin. It can also be manufactured synthetically from coal tar.

Coniferous Notes

Coniferous notes are obtained from juniper, spruce, pine and other similar trees. They give a creation a natural feel and are more commonly used in masculine scents.

Cuir de Russie (or Russian Leather)

Cuir de Russie refers to a specific style of scent first created by Ernest Beaux for Chanel in 1924. The leather notes in the base are derived from labdanum and birch tar, it is given a specific sweetness from rose and jasmine contrasted by the dry freshness of orange blossom. The accord is now used mainly in masculine creations.

Dry

Dry is a term used to describe a material or a scent's odour which is not sweet; in the same way wines are described as sweet or dry. These materials are generally mossy and woody in nature.

Earthy

Earthy is a term which suggests naturalness and being in touch with the earth. The best material for this is Patchouli which can smell like wet ground.

Eau de Cologne (or Kölnishwasser)
Eau de Cologne has two distinct perfumery meanings.

a. style of fragrance created in the town of Cologne in Germany from which it takes its name. It was created at the beginning of the 18th century by an Italian named Paul Feminis who called it L'Eau admirable. At the beginning of the 19th century it was modified by a descendant named Jean Farina. Then in 1862 the formula was acquired by Roger & Gallet who modified it again and called it Jean Marie Farina. A German banker named Mühlens also created a version of the earlier product and named it 4711.

b. strength of fragrance. One that is very light, containing around 3% perfume oils. Most feminine fragrances used to come in this strength but it has now gone out of fashion. Today the term is used for some masculine fragrance strengths but there is no constancy as to what this strength refers to.

Eau de Parfum
Eau de parfum is the fragrance strength between perfume and eau de toilette; its structure means that it is slightly longer lasting than eau de toilette, with approximately 30% left after four hours.

Eau de Toilette (or Toilette Water)
Eau de toilette is the least lasting strength of fragrance in feminine perfumery. It's structure is such that some 80% will disappear within four hours. It was, and is, designed to be refreshing.

Eau Fraîche
Eau fraîche is a toilet water at a similar strength to eau de Cologne but made with higher grade alcohol.

Enfleurage
Enfleurage is one of the oldest methods known to obtain scented oils. It works on the principle that fat absorbs odour – you would never put fish next to butter in a fridge as it would absorb the smell. Flowers are placed on odourless fat, removed and replaced until the fat is saturated with oil. At this stage the fat is known as pomade. The fat is then processed to remove the oil, known as an absolute. This method is rarely practiced today as it is very labour intensive, but it is occasionally still used to process tuberose.

Essential Oil
Essential oils are obtained from many types of plants and flowers. They are extremely volatile and are obtained by steam distillation or in the case of citrus fruits through a method called expression.

Expression
Expression is the method reserved for the citrus family - mechanical crushers literally squeeze the oil from the rind where the oil is found.

Extraction (or Solvent Extraction)
Solvent extraction is used to obtain oil from a vast number of plants and flowers. The material being treated is placed inside a large container which has perforated trays inside and allows the solvent to pass easily through it. The solvent removes the oil and produces a thick waxy paste, known as a concrete, in which the oil is trapped. The concrete is then washed with alcohol to remove the unscented waxy stearoptene's, which are discarded, leaving just the oil and alcohol mixture. The alcohol is evaporated off leaving the oil known as an absolute.

Factice (or Dummy)
A factice is a bottle used for display which is filled with coloured liquid not fragrance, which can withstand the heat and light of a perfumery store.

Fixative
A fixative is an ingredient with a very low volatility that lasts well on the skin. It has the ability to make the ingredients combined with it last longer than they otherwise would. Perfume contains the highest proportion of fixatives. See also 'balsam'.

Floral
Floral is a term used to describe a fragrance with a high proportion of floral ingredients. They are generally the sweetest of all scents.

Fougère
Fougère is a term used to describe a category of fragrances traditionally based around a blend of lavender, geranium, oakmoss and coumarin. The accord was created by Houbigant in 1882 with the launch of Fougère Royale.

Fragrance Family
Fragrance family is the term used to describe a specific style or group of perfumes that have similar materials in the structure giving them a distinctive olfactory quality.

Fragrance Foundation
The Fragrance Foundation was formed in America in 1948 to promote the public understanding of fragrance thereby increasing their enjoyment and, ultimately, the amount they use and purchase. It has now become an international organisation which holds an awards ceremony known as the FiFi's to recognise excellence within the industry.

Galbanum
Galbanum is a gum resin from the giant fennel. Through steam distillation an essential oil is produced. It is leaf-like and is the main contributor to what are known as green notes.

Grasse
Grasse is a small town in the South of France that is central to the perfumery industry. Many raw materials of the finest quality grow there and many more are shipped to be processed. Traditionally the home of the fine leather industry and scented gloves, it started to develop a perfumery business when Catherine de Medici married Henri II of France and bought her perfumer with her. His name was René le Florentin and he chose to open his perfume workshop in the town because of the abundance of high quality flowers growing freely.

Green
Green is a term used to describe a leafy freshness obtained from materials such as galbanum and violet leaf. It is jargon and can cause confusion with customers. The note gives freshness, which is a better term as it cannot cause confusion.

Gum Resin
Gum resins are sticky sap-like excretions from certain trees and shrubs. See also 'balsam'.

Harmony
Perfumers blend oils to create a pleasing effect which is known as a harmony. A blend that is not harmonious is known as discordant.

Heart Note (or Middle Note)
Heart notes or middle notes are the ones which remind us most of a specific fragrance. They have a moderate lasting effect and are generally floral, fruity or spicy in character.

Herbaceous
Herbaceous materials are known as aromatic notes all of which are herbs. See 'aromatic'.

Hesperidic (Citrus or Agrumen)
Hesperidic notes are citrus notes. The term hesperidic refers to a blend of citrus materials rarely used singularly. See also 'citrus notes'.

Incense
Incense is the term used for highly fragrant materials which are burnt to release their scent. They have been known of since antiquity. Today the term is often used to refer to frankincense.

Infusion
An infusion is often referred to as a tincture. It is the name of a product produced by placing a raw material in alcohol and allowing time to pass until the alcohol has become scented. See 'tincture'.

Kyphyi / Kyphi
Kyphyi or Kyphi is the name of the sacred Egyptian perfume or oil containing a number of aromatic herbs and resins including frankincense, myrrh, juniper berries, saffron and honey, all steeped in wine.

Labdanum
Labdanum is the gum resin obtained from shrubs of the cistus genus. The resin exudes in sticky droplets on the underside of the leaves and stems and is extracted by volatile solvents. It is extremely important in modern perfumery as a fixative but also its odour closely resembles that of the highly costly ambergris. Fragrances that are referred to as having amber are often referring to labdanum. See also 'amber', 'ambergris', 'balsams', 'fixatives', and 'gum resins'.

Lavandin
Lavandin is the term given to hybrid versions of lavender which yield an inferior quality oil to that of true or garden lavender (lavandula angustifolia) which is grown in England and the south of France.

Leather Notes
Leather notes is the term applied to certain ingredients that add a sensual, leather-like quality, such as birch and labdanum. Their odour is slightly woody, tarry and smoky. They are used most often in Chypré fragrances.

Mace & Nutmeg
Mace is the wrapping around the kernal of the fruit from the nutmeg tree; the kernal or nut itself is nutmeg.

Maceration

Maceration is a very old method in which the material being treated is placed in boiling oil or fat to remove the oils. The process is quite brutal and has generally been replaced. But it is still used to obtain certain oils from specific ingredients.

Marine Note

Marine notes or the marine accord is usually the synthetic ingredient called calone. This molecule is used widely in many new creations, particularly masculine ones, to give a feeling of freshness reminiscent of the sea.

Mossy Note

Moss notes are obtained from mosses, oakmoss being the finest and certain wood notes that have mossy aspects such as patchouli.

Muguet

Muguet is the french word for the flower lily of the valley.

Narcotic

Narcotic is a term used to describe intense materials such as jasmine, tuberose, hyacinth and animal notes which present an addictive rich sensuality.

Notes

Notes are the name given to each ingredient or group of ingredients within a fragrance composition.

Oceanic

Oceanic fragrances evoke the feeling of the sea and the seashore but without actually smelling like them. They are sometimes also referred to as ozonic.

Opoponax

Opoponax is a gum resin that closely resembles myrrh.

Orris

Orris is the bulb or rhizome of the iris. It is not a floral note. Orris gives a luxurious powdery quality to a fragrance.

Parfum or Perfume

Parfum or Perfume Also known as extrait or extract. Perfume is the perfect expression of a fragrance. It is soft and long-lasting – some 50% of its structure will last for approximately 24 hours. Perfume takes its name from the latin, per fumum, which means 'through smoke', as the earliest fragrances were burnt in the form of incense to release their odour.

Perfumers Organ

The perfumers organ is a piece of furniture somewhat like a desk with tiered shelves around three sides on which are placed the oils used by the perfumer. The unusual name comes from the fact that the bottles look a little like the stops on a church organ.

Pomade

Pomade is a thick waxy paste, similar to a concrete, which is created as a result of enfleurage.

Resinoïd

Resinoïds are dry materials that are immersed in alcohol to retrieve the oils contained within them. The gum resins are treated this way.

Sillage

Sillage is a French word that means 'track' or 'wake', which in perfumery, is the aroma left behind by a person wearing perfume as they pass by. The term trail is also used.

Smoky Note

A term used to describe a smoky or leathery effect often obtained from birch tar oil.

Synthetic

Synthetic is a term used to describe odiferous materials that are created in the laboratory. These materials are often used to recreate the complex natural odour of a physical item (usually a flower, which is often impossible or hard to extract an oil from) such as lily of the valley. Alternatively they are simple odiferous molecules – as in the case of calone, which gives us the so-called marine note.

Tincture

Tincture is the term applied to a product produced by placing a raw material in alcohol. Over time the scented oil will leave the raw material and dissolve leaving a mixture or alcohol and oil. The solvent is usually then removed.

Unguent

Unguents are the semi-solid perfumed ointment or grease made by steeping fragrant plants into animal fat. See also 'enfleurage'.

123
456
789

THE PERFUME HOUSES

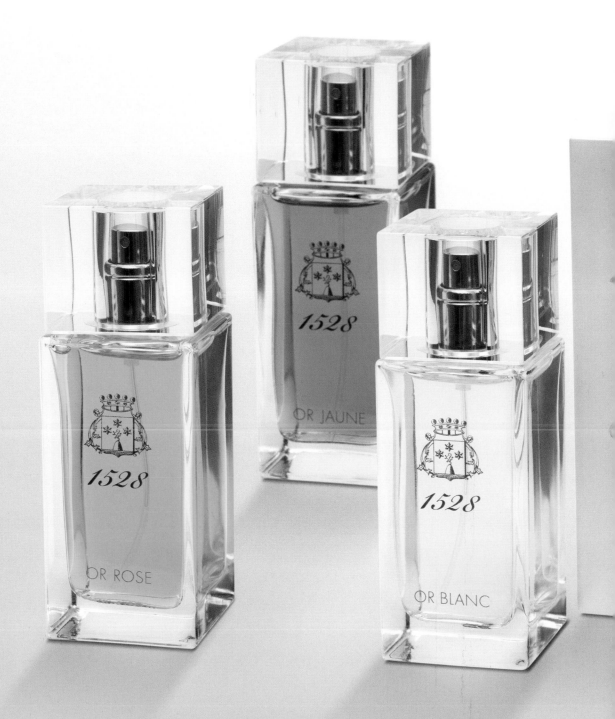

1528 PARFUMS

1528 Parfums is a modern perfume brand inspired by the spirit of the medieval Italian tradition of alchemy and the exotic materials brought back by travellers in ancient times. It all started back in 1395 in the Italian city of Genoa when a local religious figure, Giovanni-Battista, started creating perfume formulas. His love and understanding of alchemy was reflected in the scents he created based on precious materials and their natural energy. There was a great sense of 'universal spirit' in Giovanni-Battista's creations – of nature colliding with the metaphysical. When his documents were discovered years later in a hidden drawer, time had yellowed them a little but essentially they were intact. The year was 1528 when these creations were brought to light and enjoyed to their full merit. Today their creator's philosophy and craftsmanship; the beauty and quality of the essences he used have been re-introduced and re-interpreted for a modern audience. The opportunity for their new lease of life came about through a fortuitous collaboration with the Italian gold leaf conceptual artist Anna Carla de Leonardis.

The trio of scents that make up 1528 Parfums today was designed to interpret Anna Carla's vision of art and creativity. More abstract in their depiction of the actual smell of gold, these wonderful fragrances are named after three forms of the precious metal and are called: Or Blanc (White Gold), Or Rose (Pink Gold) and Or Jaune (Yellow Gold). They contain spices, plants, woods and flowers that would have been brought back at the time of the great explorers.

Each scent captures powerful and sensual tones in keeping with the magic of alchemy. Starting with Yellow Gold – a golden ray of sunshine emanating with delicate orange blossom and bergamot, and warmth with jasmine, tree moss, amber and vanilla. Its accents are enveloping, deeply sensual and reminiscent of leather. Yellow Gold, like all of the range is perfect for both men and women.

White Gold is a seductive blend of aromatic basil, lavender, patchouli, tree moss and sandalwood with undertones of tobacco that calm the senses and offer a gentle balance to the headier notes of Yellow Gold. If however, richer fragrances are more your thing, the devastating Pink Gold should please with the sweetness of cloves and lilac and the powdery softness of violet and iris. Add to this generous helpings of intoxicating tuberose (known for its aphrodisiac qualities), jasmine and vanilla, and the result comes close to chocolate – wicked but practically irresistible!

If you haven't yet had the chance to smell these complex and delicious fragrances, they are the perfect excuse for a trip to Italy to dip into this sumptuous world of olfactory luxury. The story of 1528 Parfums tells of ancient tradition meeting innovation and passion head on. The outcome is spectacular.

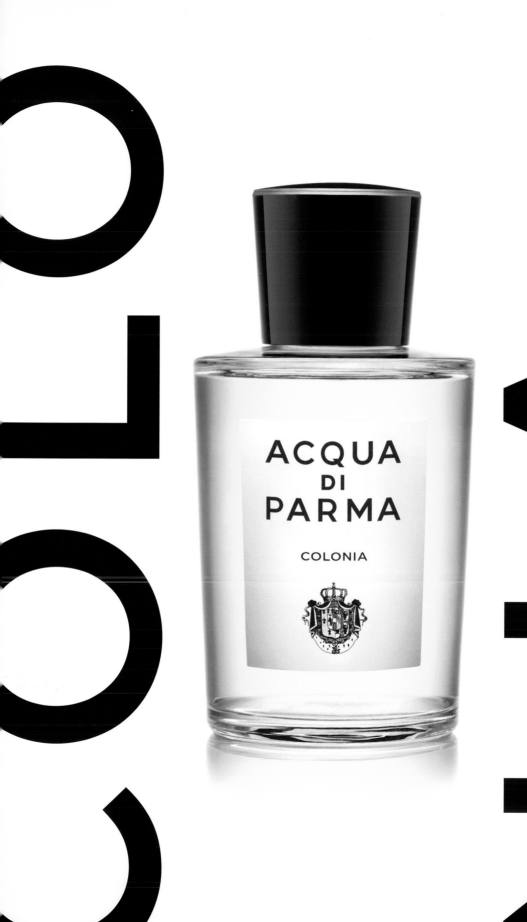

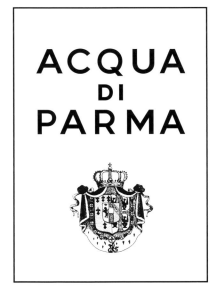

LA COLONIA ITALIANA

Acqua di Parma Colonia is where the legend began. It is the olfactory archetype which, in all its rich nuances, conveys the essence of being Italian. This triumph of *haute parfumerie* is expressed in two more recent and harmonious variations on the fragrance – Colonia Assoluta and Colonia Intensa.

The Acqua di Parma story began in 1916 with a small factory of essences in the ancient heart of Parma, the city of Giuseppe Verdi and Stendhal. It was here, with their visionary sensibility, that these master perfumers created an unusually refreshing, crisp and subtle fragrance – Acqua di Parma Colonia – in total contrast to the intense perfumes in vogue at the time. Acqua di Parma was, and still is, created with essences, extracts and oils in a small perfumery workshop. Its sophisticated alchemy was an instant success and would soon become a timeless classic. Almost 100 years on, the formula for the fragrance has remained unchanged and its individual ingredients are still distilled by hand. Colonia Assoluta and Colonia Intensa were born of the same skill and passion.

The three varieties of Acqua di Parma Colonia are amongst the finest examples of vintage meeting contemporary in a fragrance. In this refined art of *haute parfumerie*, the classic structure of the eau de Cologne finds its expression in the citrus fruit top notes; the floral middle notes beautifully set with spices and herbs and rounded off by woody base notes.

The most important elements are the citrus fruits, which in Italy are renowned for their outstanding quality. Acqua di Parma prides itself on selecting only the finest varieties such as bergamot from Calabria, lemon and orange from Sicily, along with orange blossoms and petitgrain. Special extraction methods such as pressing the fruit peel to obtain the precious essential oil are just one of the distinguishing characteristics of this refined perfume house. It's no coincidence that Cary Grant and Audrey Hepburn among many other glamorous and dedicated admirers, have fallen for this delicate, sophisticated and irresistibly fresh scent.

A second and crucial feature is the remarkable bottle design of the Colonia and all its varieties. The celebrated Art Deco bottle created in 1916, with its sleek, contemporary lines and Bakelite lid, has become the distinctive mark of the house's fragrances across the board and has achieved iconic status for its sensual lines and unmistakable simplicity. Skilful craftsmanship is revealed in every last detail, from the labels featuring the royal blazon of Parma – each still individually applied by hand – to the handcrafted 'waffled' feature of the cylinder shaped box, in the characteristic yellow of Acqua di Parma. The labels and lids feature colours evoking the mood of each fragrance: black and white for Colonia, silver for Colonia Assoluta and bronze for Colonia Intensa.

The stylishness and elegance of Acqua di Parma means that it has no need for ostentation and remains a product which has been designed exclusively for a cosmopolitan public. Its flawless reputation endures to this day and will, no doubt, continue to spawn generations of loyal admirers in times to come.

AMOUAGE

Founded over 25 years ago to reflect the wonderful heritage and tradition of perfumery, Amouage is a niche luxury fragrance house that draws inspiration from its birthplace of the Sultanate of Oman. Devoted to creating finely blended perfumes with the highest quality of ingredients sourced from around the world, Amouage brings real artistry to the olfactory world.

The Amouage perfumes are created by internationally recognised perfumers in Grasse, in the south of France, under the guidance of company Creative Director Christopher Chong. The collection celebrates the spirit of the Orient in its use of sensual materials – not least rare silver frankincense – and ornate presentation. There is a sense that flawless quality, authenticity and the desires and aspirations of fragrance enthusiasts are the key to Amouage's wonderful scents. No room for market trends here. The distinctive house signature at the heart of each fragrance conjures a palpable feeling of luxury throughout each individual scent.

Gold, Dia, Ciel Reflection, Silver, Ubar, Jubilation, Lyric and the more recent Epic, inspired by the legendary Silk Road. The portfolio is as rich as it is varied. The striking characteristic in all of the house's fragrances is their ability to feel like a second skin – a tailor-made suit.

Take Gold – both the men's and the women's are gloriously powdery and musky, with a slightly duskier slant to the men's, thanks to patchouli and oak moss. The woman's version is silky, floral and yet inherently spicy. It feels like a familiar cashmere sweater; sophisticated and cosy all at once. Quite a feat! It contains greatly prized materials, frankincense along with myrrh, rock rose and orris, and together they leave such a fragrant veil on the skin that it's hard to remain indifferent.

Equally impossible to ignore is Jubilation which celebrates the 25th anniversary of the house of Amouage. Jubilation XXV for men is balanced but daring; surprising us with rose, orchid and the smoky warmth of gaiac wood. It unravels seamlessly like a fine wine or an intricately perfect symphony; every rewarding layer building on the next. For women, Jubilation 25 is wonderfully elegant and enigmatic. Rose and ylang-ylang move delicately around the finest frankincense from Oman with amber, musk, vetiver and patchouli. It's a remarkable fragrance.

There is also a new addition to the house portfolio with the exclusive Library Collection. A tribute to the fragrances of the 1920s and 1930s, the collection makes no gender distinction and is destined to be the envy of perfume houses the world over as it pays homage to one of the most elegant periods of the last hundred years.

As if these olfactory treats weren't enough, loyal followers and newcomers alike can also take pleasure from a gorgeously scented bath and body collection with sumptuous gels, soaps and ultra nourishing creams. So far Gold, Dia, Reflection for men and women, Jubilation and Lyric for women have their own bath line. A home collection of candles and *parfums d'ambiance* (interior fragrances) also complements the existing fragrances alongside nine new purposely created scents. As one of the most luxurious perfume houses on the planet with more than thirty countries now carrying the collection in world class stores, there is no excuse not to discover the olfactory heaven that is Amouage.

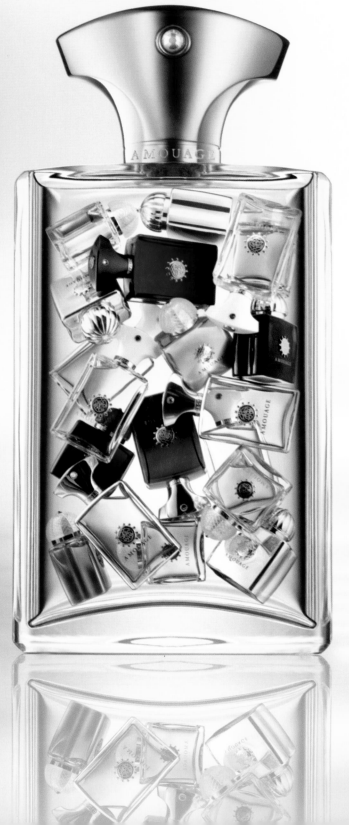

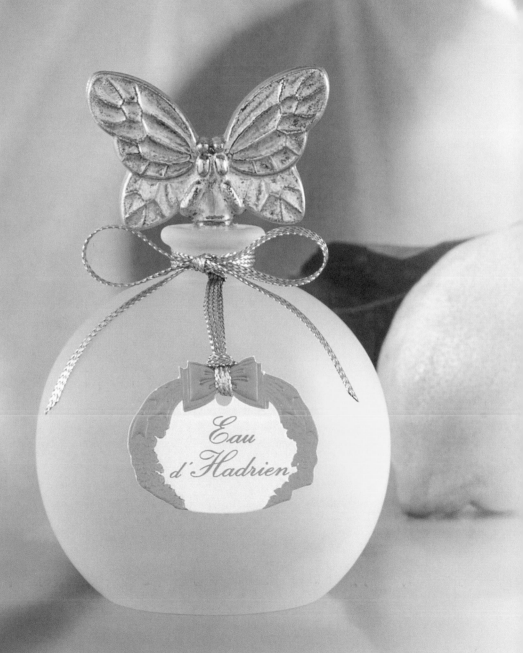

ANNICK GOUTAL

Annick Goutal, previously a prize-winning concert pianist and fashion model, had a chance encounter with perfumer Henri Sorsana in 1977 that was to change her destiny forever. She had been creating skin creams with a friend but felt they lacked beautiful packaging and fragrance. Annick then started experimenting with perfume ingredients. She discovered she had a natural ability for hitting the right notes and in 1981 Eau d'Hadrien was born. Charming bottles, inspired by antique glassware, were then created for her fragrances. Each one of these was (and still is) hand finished with a perfect little bow and a delicate label. Annick Goutal became synonymous with Eau d'Hadrien, a stunning success and still the symbol of the brand today. With its quintessentially Mediterranean character it perfectly evokes sun drenched gardens lined with cypress trees, bursting with sparkling citrus and grapefruit. Annick went on to dedicate this composition to her beloved husband, the celebrated musician Alain Meunier.

Unashamedly romantic and imaginative, Annick Goutal is known for creating deeply personal fragrant symphonies that unfold like love stories and are inspired by true relationships and real life experiences.

When Annick Goutal's life came to a sad and premature end at the age of just 53, she had already created a legacy of 19 stunning fragrances. Perhaps appropriately, and almost by a romantic twist of fate, one of these fragrances (arguably the most enduring of all her fragrant 'tales') is the one she created for her young daughter Camille – Petite Chérie or 'Little Darling'. It smells of pear drops and is quite simply mouth-watering as it celebrates Camille's youthful beauty and character.

With time and the passing of her mother, Camille's beauty flourished as did her passion for photography and fragrance. She now continues to write her own fragrant melodies, creating perfumes inspired, like her mother, by love, moments in time and memorable places such as the island of Ile de Ré where her family share memories of many happy vacations.

Through a fortuitous fusion of minds Camille has forged an incredible partnership with Isabelle Doyen, a most respected nose who'd previously worked with Annick. Their connection has led to stunning new fragrances. Their love of Asia, for example, is reflected in Un Matin d'Orage – an ode to a storm drenched Japanese garden as the earth begins to warm in the morning sun. It is an invitation to walk through that garden with the rain soaked gardenia to hand…

Each fragrance tells a tale as unique as the last. There's the wonderfully fruity floral Quel Amour! created as an homage to love, it is the ultimate celebration of femininity with its peony, rose and cranberry. Then there's the luscious Les Nuits d'Hadrien which beautifully interprets warm Tuscan nights in a symphony of cypress, basil and cumin with rich ylang-ylang and vanilla. Depth and contrast has gradually defined the collection and the arrival of Ninfeo mio is a wonderful illustration of this. The breathtaking garden Giardino di Ninfa, near Rome, is the modern day garden of Eden that inspired Ninfeo mio with its beautiful aromas. The result is a deliciously languorous yet sparkling fragrance for men and women that blends milky smooth fig, herbaceous notes and lemon wood. If only all gardens could smell just like this. For those who seek timeless elegance; who simply love to be in love, make no apologies and let yourself be swept into the universe of Annick Goutal.

AQABA

Thousands of years ago King Solomon's legendary love for the Queen of Sheba flourished on the sands of Aqaba. Aqaba is a jeweled city on an ancient caravan route upon which luxurious cargoes of gold, perfumes and fine silks passed.

In this city, amidst all that was precious, the Queen of Sheba famously captured the heart of a monarch and became his cherished Queen. Out of love for Sheba, King Solomon built fleets of ships to bring her incense, aromatic oils and spices from far east kingdoms in India and China.

AQABA, the gloriously sensual signature fragrance for women inspired by this historical setting is accompanied by AQABA MEN which draws on the passion, power and perfection of man. All the house's creations stem from deeply romantic themes and the fragrance AQABA Spring continues this homage – its delicate ode to eternal love, based on luscious green notes. Further capturing Sheba's lust for adventure, courage and curiosity is the recent Jewels of AQABA collection (an extension of AQABA Spring) which includes Sands, Blu and Midnight Sun. These fragrances celebrate the beauty of Mother Nature. AQABA represents the search for a single link embracing the embodiment of ancient and modern worlds. A product of years of research by Miriam Mirani and her collaboration with Firmenich's Thierry Wasser; the fragrance came to life in 1998. She had, herself, led a life that exposed her to worlds past and present; Mirani was born to parents whose cultures comprised traditions from Eastern Europe and the Mediterranean. She spent her formative years in the cultural capital of Salzburg, Austria, the Middle East and America. Her music studies were nurtured at the Eastman School of Music and the Mozarteum Conservatory in Salzburg. At the age of 20 however, her eagerness to learn about the outside world became a pressing priority and it was at this point she felt compelled to embark upon her lengthy odyssey.

Armed with the fruits of her rigorous research into age-old civilizations, their languages and history, Mirani travelled south through Egypt's desert oasis, journeyed with the Bedouins and fell in love with the colours and magic of the Sinai Desert and Nile Delta. At the tip of the Red Sea, clear to the eye, lay the cornerstones of the ancient world and the jewel of AQABA tucked neatly in its centre. The impression would last forever.

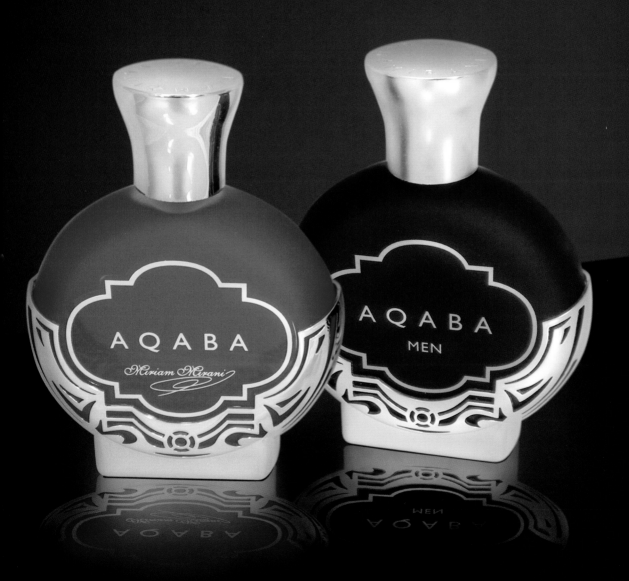

ARAMIS

Launched in 1964, Aramis became an overnight success with men looking for something deeper and more compelling in their fragrance, as well as with women who couldn't resist smelling it! With a complete line of convincing and professional products made exclusively for men, Aramis created a revolution in the men's grooming market. Much to the excitement of their girlfriends and wives, it quickly became acceptable and virile for men to take care of their appearance and wear fragrance on a daily basis.

The name 'Aramis' was taken from an exotic Turkish root known to hold aphrodisiac properties. This is quite apt given the effect it can have on anyone who smells it. Aramis has stood the test of time with elegant packaging, a distinctive fragrant character and universal appeal across the generations. Elegant, sophisticated and unmistakably masculine its accomplished scent is like a fine scotch whisky that's been macerating in a barrel of the finest spices. It conjures images of a cosy library creaking with worldly leather bound books, warmed by an open fire and the aroma of cigars. Or the mossy, earthy forest floor on a crisp autumn day. There's an intangible quality of depth, reassurance and timelessness that has captured the imagination of thousands of perfume lovers for over 40 years. It's a wonderful chypré fragrance in all its glory with bergamot, clary sage, patchouli and tree moss. With subtle and varied moods it evokes an irresistible appeal – it's easy to understand why this contemporary fragrance is as relevant today as ever.

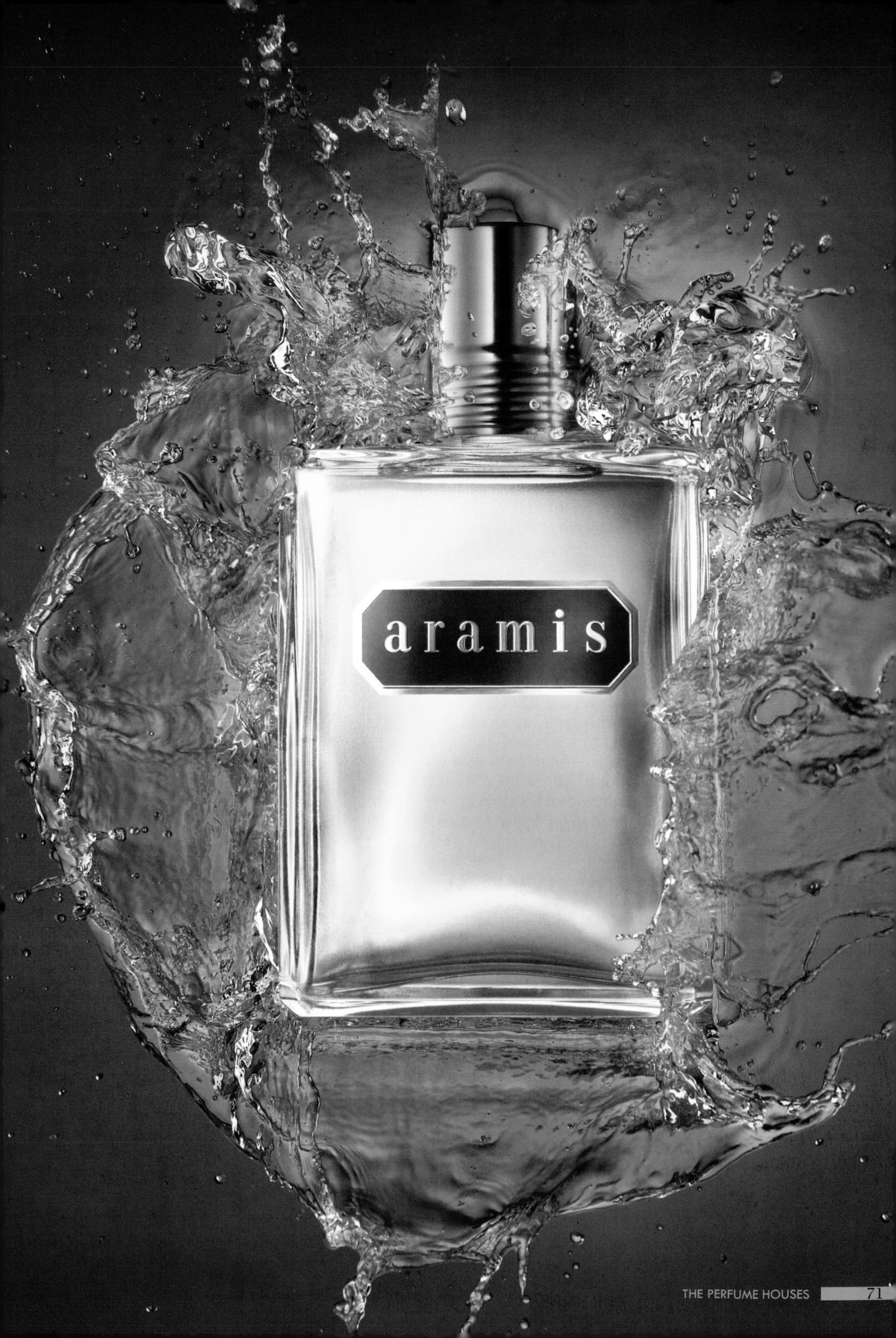
aramis

BIEHL PARFUMKUNSTWERKE

Thorsten Biehl, an internationally respected fragrance expert with almost 20 years of experience in the perfume industry, has astutely drawn upon some expert 'perfume noses' to create in his 'olfactory gallery'. Six fascinating perfumers have produced their perfumes for biehl parfumkunstwerke without the usual constraints of market research, marketing or the need to maximise profits and the end result has naturally yielded a collection of extraordinary fragrances.

The simplicity of using the perfumer's initials to name each scent with an index number is all part of the scheme: "My focus is always on the work and the artist behind it", explains Thorsten Biehl. For the bottle and packaging, for example, he opted for a luxurious yet minimalist design, letting the scent speak for itself; standard transparent 100ml glass bottles show the company logo and the perfume initials and number. Exclusivity and quality take priority and thanks to this beautiful collection the wearer's personality can take centre stage.

Henning Biehl: Elegant
Henning Biehl juxtaposes contrast with harmony. The natural and fantasy components he uses do more than blend together – they're like musical notes in an impressive symphony celebrating femininity and elegance. Henning Biehl created the magical hb01 scent in the biehl parfumkunstwerke gallery.

Mark Buxton: Provocative

It all started with a blind fragrance test on TV. Despite losing the contest, Mark Buxton's talent was discovered and he was subsequently offered the chance to train as a perfumer at the Haarmann & Reimer perfume company. Now Paris based, he is one of only a handful of people who can actually identify and name a few thousand perfume notes. He modestly maintains that the only way to train well in the art of smelling is to discuss it. Mark Buxton created the cool and erotic mb01; the relaxed and sophisticated mb02 and finally the wonderfully deep mb03.

Patricia Choux: Unconventional

Patricia Choux had dreamed of being a perfume creator since she was a child and her admission to the renowned ISIPCA school for perfumers in Paris was the first step towards fulfilling her dream. Her training in Paris was followed by years of training with Symrise in Holzminden, Germany's largest fragrance company, and then further assignments as a perfumer in London, Paris and New York, where she has been living and working since 2005. Her style is bold, crazy and chic. Landscapes, colours, smells and cultures endlessly inspire her fresh and exciting fragrances. She likes to experiment with exotic notes, in particular her favourite flower, jasmine. Patricia Choux created the sunny and airy pc01 and the vibrant and cheerful pc02.

Egon Oelkers: Refined

Egon Oelker's work as a perfumer has taken him to Cannes, New York, Geneva, Paris, Hamburg and Asia. He is particularly fond of the Far East and its abundance of spices, exotic fruits and rare woods perfectly captured in many of his fragrances. His wonderful career started almost 40 years ago as a graduate chemist when he trained as a perfumer with the long-established Haarmann & Reimer company in Holzminden. He has since gone on to train some of today's most respected and successful perfumers. He is noted and admired for his discreet, luxurious fragrances and finds much of his inspiration from mountain hikes. Egon Oelkers created the warming eo01; the classic eo02 and the extravagant eo03.

Arturetto Landi: Opulent

Arturetto Landi is a chemist by profession, he was drawn into the world of perfume by chance. After graduating he wanted to learn English and work at sea, so he moved to England. His destiny changed when he landed a casual job with a scent company and discovered a talent for fragrance. Landi's perfumes are opulent, complex and composed like a grand opera for the nose. He grew up on the Italian Riviera where his father was a professional chef. Landi also developed a fascination for Arabian scents and distant lands. All these factors have contributed to his sensual style of fragrance creations. Arturetto Landi has created two perfumes in the gallery: the elegant and refined al01 and the seductive al02.

Geza Schoen: Rebellious

Less is more in Geza's universe. Where others might blend hundreds of essences, Geza Schoen restricts himself to a small selection of top quality raw materials. The decision is founded on experience and he feels that using fewer components makes for more impressive creations. Shunning the mainstream he has carved himself an exclusive niche in the perfume world. At the age of 13 he could already identify over 100 male fragrances blindfolded. His career choice was clear. Born in Kassel and now living in Berlin, Geza is one of only 30 or so perfumers in Germany with traditional training yet radical ideas. For Thorsten Biehl, Geza Schoen created the deep yet clear gs01 and the erotic gs02.

Bulgari has always stood for sophistication and style in every aspect of its creative work. Andy Warhol once likened the experience of entering a Bulgari boutique to visiting a world class contemporary art exhibition. When Bulgari was originally founded in 1884 by Sotirio Bulgari, it was known for its work with silver in brooches and then much later as a jeweller. A fascination with beauty and elegance made the progression into luxury fragrances a natural one which balanced classical inspiration with constant creative research. A keen eye for detail and perfection led this family business to approach Jean-Claude Ellena, whose previous olfactory masterpieces would guarantee success and integrity. So it was, that in 1993 Bulgari launched Ellena's now legendary Eau Parfumée au Thé Vert. This exhilarating fragrance was inspired by Ellena's serious love of the fine teas he and his wife would regularly savour at Mariages Frères in Paris. The teas triggered the sketching of countless

olfactory landscapes in his mind. The result is a stylised interpretation that accentuates tea's vibrant, refreshing notes and came to define Ellena's style – clean, intellectual, minimalist yet soulful – often copied but never matched. Bulgari's move into fragrance proved to be incredibly successful and to this day the fragrances have remained relevant thanks to the use of a wide range of different creators with distinctive styles.

Bulgari pour Femme and pour Homme launched in 1994 and 1995 respectively explore a wealth of rich and precious materials which perfectly reflect Bulgari's clientele. The fragrances are considered contemporary classics. Their success prompted Bulgari to re-launch them in a modern context alongside the new Voile de Jasmin and Rose Essentielle for women; Pour Homme Extrême and Pour Homme Soir for men.

With such timeless gems in their portfolio you could be mistaken for thinking that Bulgari's fragrances remain resolutely traditional. Not so; Black in 1998 and Omnia in 2003 heralded a master stroke in reinvention for the new millennium. The Black fragrance could easily fit into any daring, niche perfumer's collection with its dark, smoky undertones and urban edge. Similarly, Omnia turned the oriental concept of fragrance on its head by incorporating fresher notes along with sweeter touches of almond, chocolate and cinnamon. The overall effect was lighter and more modern sensuality. This spirit of innovation and an

BVLGARI

innate ability to gauge shifts in perfume tastes continued in 2005 with Aqua pour Homme – a vibrant masculine scent, awash with richly aquatic notes and fragrant orange groves – which has become one of Bulgari's most popular fragrances. With its starkly contrasting notes the fragrance BlV II also embraces change without neglecting the legacy left by its predecessors.

Next time you catch a glimpse of the Bulgari double logo, be sure to take time to discover the hidden depths of this collection. You'll be surprised at how unique and breathtaking the contemporary classic has become.

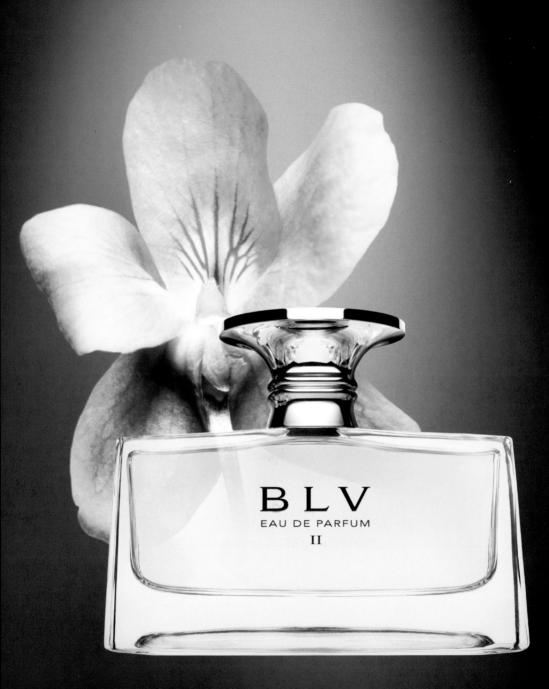

CALYX

Close your eyes and put your nose to the dreamy scent that is Calyx. In the bottle it hints at the freshness lying in the top notes. On the skin it positively glows with a vibrancy and crispness that is quite breathtaking. Blue skies, the buzz of the cicadas, fruit cocktails and lazy days in the Mediterranean sunshine – the snapshot is vividly sketched as the scent releases its green and fruity top notes. Created in 1986, the years have only served to preserve the youthful joy of this exhilarating composition. Given the delicate, intelligent balance of sharp and soft; the blend of fruit and flowers, musk and woods, it comes as no surprise that one of the greatest perfumers of all time, Sophia Grojsman, composed it. Named after the leaf-like outer protective covering of a flower, Calyx reverses the usual rules of perfume. The top notes are big, emphatic and lively – juicy mandarin, passion fruit, guava and mango – softening as they develop to sophisticated lily, jasmine and rose before settling on comforting moss, cedar and musk.

Sophia was inspired to create Calyx after a trip to the Mediterranean to visit a friend. Upon her arrival she was engulfed by an overwhelming fragrance. As she opened the window to her bedroom to take in the view of the garden, she realised she was surrounded by orange blossoms and grapefruit – the extraordinary perfume mesmerised her. The fragrance was overpowering and Sophia worried she may not be able to sleep so she closed the window. The next morning the scent was all around her, however, she realised that she felt more refreshed and energised than she ever did before. It was then that she knew she had to recreate this compelling fragrance for others to enjoy and experience.

Calyx is a remarkable fragrance. It's playful and happy, yet seductive and complex that lingers for hours and hours. It's a tonic to the senses and remains as relevant today as when it burst onto the fragrance scene almost a quarter of a century ago. Calyx is for women with spirit and independence who leave a trace of their scent behind them and an indelible impression in the memories of all those lucky enough to get close. It is a true cult classic.

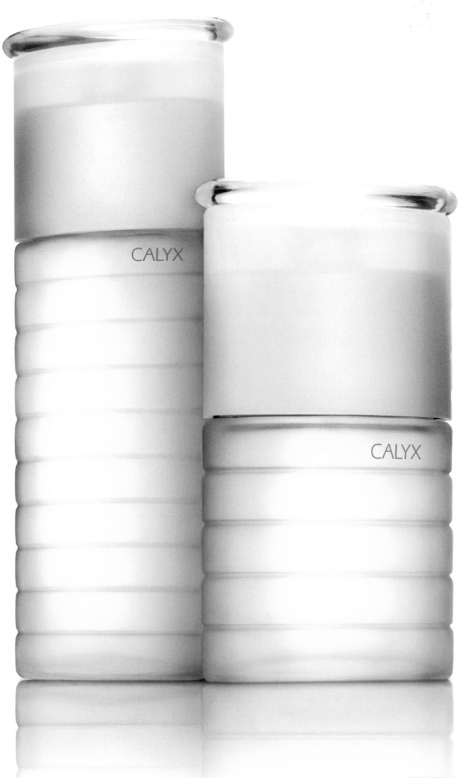

CHRISTIAN DIOR

highest level of artistry. Only the best, the most luxurious of ingredients, were suitable to enter the composition of his perfumes.

His devotion to fragrance resulted in constant creativity and in some of the most celebrated scents of the last century. Working with Edmond Roudnitska, Christian Dior released truly ground breaking and timeless perfumes such as Eau Fraîche a unisex fragrance launched in 1953, and the masterpiece Diorissimo in 1956, for which he personally designed the jewel bottle. True to this heritage of quality and excellence, Christian Dior's legacy lived on after his death in 1957 with the creation of emblematic fragrances such as the timeless Eau Sauvage in 1966 and Poison and Fahrenheit in the 1980s.

Christian Dior grew up surrounded by the scents of the garden at his family home in Granville; a floral oasis of roses, camellias and lily of the valley that formed the couturier's olfactory background and was a constant source of inspiration. For him a couture dress was unimaginable without the finishing touch of femininity – fragrance. This passion was embodied by his first collection in 1947, when his "New Look" was unveiled alongside his first fragrance, the iconic Miss Dior. From this point on he dedicated himself to creating fragrances that echoed the beauty of his couture dresses emerging from the bottle one by one.

An artisan at heart, Christian Dior wished for his perfumes to be made with the same perfectionist care and uncompromising standards as his dresses. He felt that "true luxury demands the finest materials and the finest craftsmanship," and feeling, "as much a perfumer as a couturier" he took perfume to the

In 1999 a new legend was born with the launch of J'adore Eau de Parfum, a unique fragrance that expresses the absolute femininity and essence of the Dior couture spirit. The opulent fruity-floral juice takes flight with a fresh accord of bergamot opening into a vibrant armful of roses and delicate jasmine sambac. It is followed by plum, sensuous and honey-like with a caress of tuberose. John Galliano inspired the bottle, designed by Hervé Van der Straeten, crowning the amphora with a headdress in tribute to the Massai necklaces of his first haute couture collection. An instant perfumery classic since 2004, the fragrance has boasted Charlize Theron as its ambassador representing glamour, strength, elegance and talent – the perfect icon for J'adore.

Today the House of Dior's fragrances rest in the hands of Dior Perfumer François Demachy, with the composition of scents such as Miss Dior Chérie L'Eau, Dior Homme Sport and Les Escales de Dior. François Demachy was always destined for a life of fragrance, having spent his childhood in the fragrance heartland of Grasse. His father ran a pharmacy and counted the legendary perfumer Edmond Roudnitska among his clients. François Demachy uses his expertise and artist's sensitivity to pursue the legacy of the Dior *savoir faire*. In his quest for excellence and luxury he has founded the Dior Fragrance Creation Laboratory. It is, as François describes it, "the place where ideas are born and take their actual shape." Research begins here. In this respect it is true to the spirit of Monsieur Dior, who saw his house as a creative space in perpetual activity, "where the only thing that mattered was the sacred fire of creation."

Fragrance images photographed by Philippe Schlienger.

The story of Clive Christian Perfumes begins over a century ago in 1872, when Queen Victoria acknowledged the superior quality of the Crown Perfumery fragrances. She granted the image of her crown to sit on every bottle as an enduring symbol of British quality and excellence.

It's fair to say that British luxury designer Clive Christian has breathed new life into the luxury perfume business. Christian had purchased the historic Crown Perfumery in 1999 and had been inspired by one of the vintage scents to release his first fragrance under his own name. This fragrance was 1872 (named for the year the Crown Perfumery was established), it marked the beginning of a new millennium and a new era for luxury perfumes.

In 2002 he discontinued the Crown line, but has continued to release new fragrances – pure perfumes – under the Clive Christian label, including the aforementioned 1872; No1 (advertised as 'the world's most expensive perfume') and X. This wonderful revival and homage to the essence of great British luxury and perfume heralds a return to the original values of the highly concentrated and complex formulas of the Crown Perfumery.

To achieve superior quality blends no expense has been spared in the creation of Clive Christian perfumes. Each individual scent contains the rarest and most precious natural ingredients available and oozes sophistication. The moment they touch your skin you know you're in for a wonderful olfactory experience. There is a fragrance for men and one for women in each of the Clive Christian scents. They are composed of the most precious woods, flowers and spices. 1872 plays on freshness, nature and green notes for men and fruity floral notes for women; X explores the depths of oriental notes for men and mossy spices for women – perfect for evening wear. And No1 celebrates oriental flowers for women and rich woods for men in all their splendour.

For Clive Christian, the design of the bottle that holds each drop of perfume is as important as the perfume itself. In addition to reviving the original spray bottles bearing Queen Victoria's crown from the perfumery archives, Clive also designed a hand cut lead crystal stopper bottle for the pure perfume aficionado. The No1 Pure Perfume bottle bears a single white brilliant cut diamond at the collar as a symbol of the rarity of the ingredients within. It's a testament to the beauty of this range that the Fragrance Foundation presented Clive Christian with a unique award recognizing 'outstanding perfume presentation' for his Baccarat 'Imperial Majesty' limited edition bottle of No1.

"X"

PERFUME CREATIO
CLIVE CHRISTIA
LONDON ENGLAN

EST 1872

CREATED USING THE RAREST AND
MOST PRECIOUS NATURAL INGREDIENTS

No1

THE WORLDS MOST
EXPENSIVE PERFUME

MMIV

CLIVE CHRISTIAN LONDON ENGLAND

1872

MADE IN ENGLAND USING THE
NATURAL INGREDIENTS AS
ORIGINALLY CREATED BY THE
CROWN PERFUMERY IN 1872

CLIVE CHRISTIAN

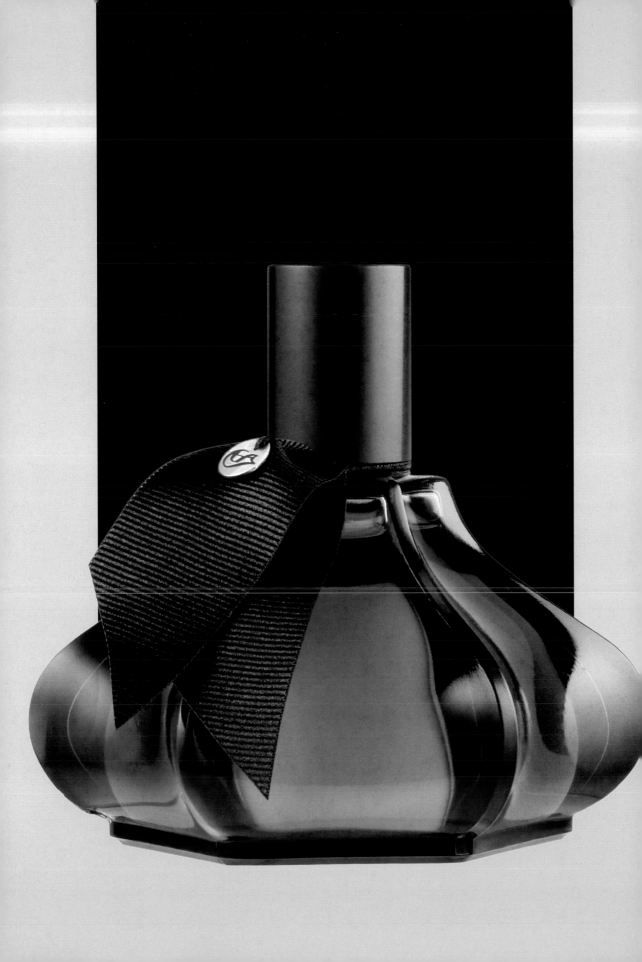

COMME DES GARÇONS

If you're searching for words to describe Comme des Garçons fragrances, 'avant-garde', 'innovative' and 'breathtaking' all spring to mind; fittingly perhaps given the global reputation of Rei Kawakubo's trendsetting company.

The first perfume, Eau de Parfum, was launched in 1994 and has been described as "a perfume that works like a medicine and behaves like a drug", because it feels addictive and raises the spirits. It is comforting, yet exotic with woody and spicy notes. The fragrance lives around Spanish labdanum, Iranian styrax and Moroccan cedarwood laced and with dark, spiky undertones: cardamom, cinnamon, black pepper, honey, rose, cloves, nutmeg, incense essence and sandalwood.

Its successor, CDG 2, was created in 1999. This perfume, presented in a silver mirror bottle, was inspired by the black Japanese sumi ink and plays on the contrast between dark and light, reflection and opacity. The lighter aspects of the scent come from aldehydes – wonderful and versatile synthetic notes topped with orange, mandarin blossom, vetiver and cumin. Absolute of Maté (an energising black tea found in the Andes), patchouli, labdanum and amber provide the darkness of the ink like quality.

Luxe Champaca, one of their most acclaimed perfumes was created to give timeless appeal with no expense spared in the choice of materials or the packaging. Named after the champaca–'the flower of all flowers' – it smells utterly luxurious and sparkles with white pepper, cardamom, champaca, white musk and iris. It is offset by the stylish black bottle and presented in a red box that unfolds its layers like a flower's petals.

Odeur 53 is not a perfume in the traditional sense as it contains no floral or plant essences. Instead, it is a totally new abstract smell – an 'anti-perfume'. The majority of the ingredients are true to nature copies of inorganic smells - volcanic rock, freshly mowed grass, clean washing drying in the wind, sand dunes,

fresh mountain air and the flash of metal. These smells have never been used before, making this an entirely new concept. Thus Odeur 53 is also a truly environmental perfume in the larger sense of the word.

Most recently, Comme des Garçons have collaborated on a new fragrance with the milliner Stephen Jones described as "a violet hitting a meteorite". The basis for the collaboration came in 1984 when Stephen Jones met Rei Kawakubo in Anchorage, Alaska, and their ensuing friendship paved the way for this most futuristic scent that is decorative, whimsical and strange. As Stephen says, "I've always wanted to create a fragrance. But there is no-one with whom I would rather be sharing the challenges of this project. I've always loved Comme des Garçons – in fact, I think I may have been the very first person in England to buy one. And my respect for Rei knows no bounds."

This spirit of innovation, collaboration and forward thinking permeates every aspect of the CDG brand and there is no doubt that they will continue to push boundaries and achieve new success in every endeavour they undertake.

DONNA KARAN COLLECTION

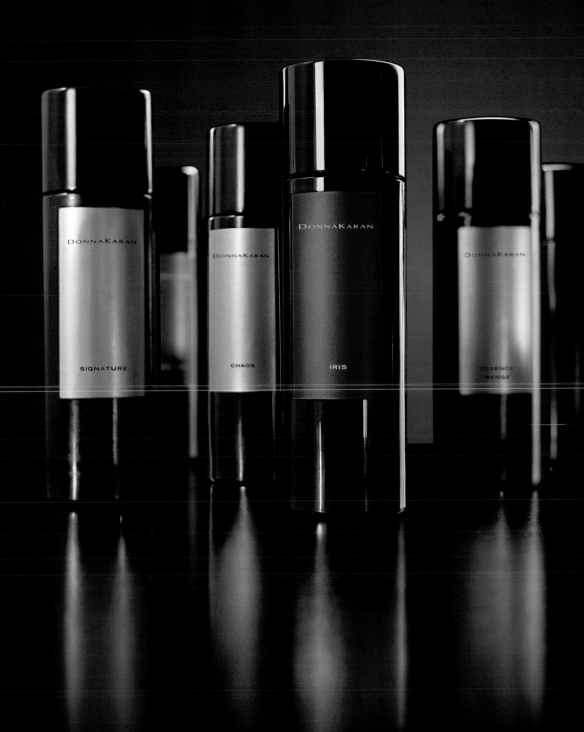

The Donna Karan Collection beautifully echoes the influential designer's iconic fashion collection. The fragrances are equally as exclusive and timeless resting seamlessly on the skin. There are eight unforgettable fragrances in the Donna Karan Collection – eight creations that befit a luxury wardrobe of scents to suit every mood and occasion. The first four are re-introductions of past and existing iconic cult compositions. They include the original seductive Donna Karan Signature scent Chaos, Fuel for Men and Black Cashmere. Donna Karan's personal favourites are the Donna Karan Essences comprising Wenge, Labdanum and Jasmine. They can be worn alone or layered to reflect a state of mind and creating a very personal aura. Finally, Iris has been recently added to the collection. Each and every one of the fragrances are designed to transcend time and fashion.

Donna Karan Signature marked the beginning of the brand's beauty range in 1992 bringing depth and warmth with sensual amber, patchouli and sandalwood. It wears its name well leaving a bewitching scented trail in its wake – the wearer's scented signature. Then Chaos, which was inspired by the designer's busy life and counteract it so effectively with its calming blend. The essence of serenity, Chaos unveils aromatic lavender, sage, coriander and chamomile with exotic woods and amber; the overall touch is velvety and comforting. These sit alongside Black Cashmere which perfectly interprets the feel of cashmere in a comforting blend of spices – cloves, nutmeg, saffron and masala spices – that conjure warmth. Fuel for Men is resolutely virile and invigorating, as the name would suggest, with musk and sensual woods.

The three Essence fragrances – Wenge, Labdanum and Jasmine offer a new dimension and are suffused with distinctly exotic notes. In turn surprising and challenging to the senses with unusual olfactory landscapes and stunning raw materials, it's important to note that they can be worn alone or together in layers. Donna Karan Wenge, one of Donna Karan's all time favourite scents celebrates exotic wenge wood native to central Africa and coveted for its artisan appeal. The wood exudes a deeply spicy aroma unlike many feminine fragrances and is utterly beguiling. Try layering it with the Labdanum fragrance to create a seriously sophisticated aura. Labdanum is a shrub resin with rich woody undertones and is perfect on men and women. Jasmine is the floral fragrance in this imaginative collection. Jasmine is a precious flower which exhales its intoxicating fragrance as the sun goes down and into the night. The essential oil extracted from jasmine is not only wonderfully fragrant but boosts feelings of wellbeing making it a favourite for sensual perfumes. Jasmine works perfectly with Labdanum for a beautifully complex mood.

Iris is the newest addition to the fragrance collection embracing the exquisite and rare iris flower producing a sensually elegant scent. Like jasmine, the iris flower is considered extremely luxurious in the production of perfume. This is mainly because the scented part of the flower is its rhizome or root, which when dried in the sun for several months can be converted to a rich substance called orris butter. The process is lengthy and yields a scent that smells like powder or violets, often used as a base to enhance a fragrance's luxurious effect.

Perfume enthusiasts are spoilt for choice with this collection. Select according to your scent style or layer two together as the mood strikes you. These Donna Karan scents are as modern as they are classic – a great fragrance never goes out of style.

EBULLIENCE

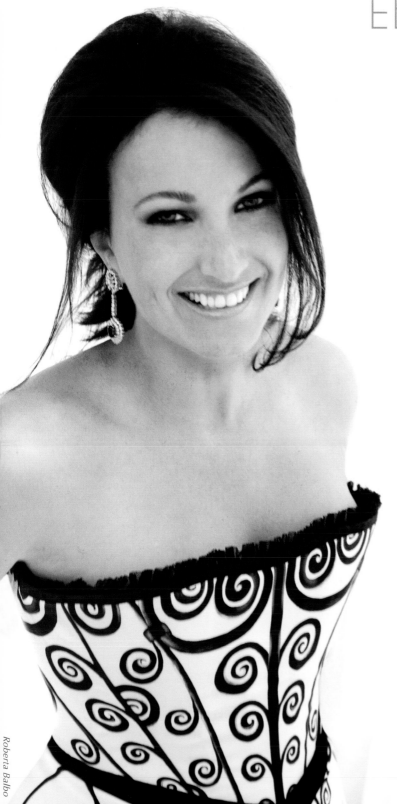

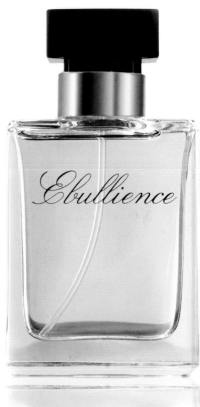

Roberta Balbo

What happens when a treasured fragrance with a quarter of a century of success under its belt teeters on the brink of disappearance? If there is such a thing as luck then a fragrant angel would sweep down to save this olfactory gem from the depths of oblivion. As fate would have it in this case, the fragrant angel was Roberta Balbo, the embodiment of refinement herself, whose mission is far more than a stroke of luck. It is a mission fired by passion and the belief that no work of art deserves to be lost to the world.

To understand the reason behind her determined effort to keep this scent alive, to breathe new life into it, we need look (and smell) no further than Roberta's upbringing. She grew up in Michigan surrounded by the fresh scents of fern, freshly cut wood, burning birch woods and mineral rich soil. Her affinity with scents reminiscent of the outdoors and of a carefree, happy existence are deep rooted and instinctive. Her greatest inspiration comes from making other people happy; it is perfectly illustrated when she says: "I love embracing Ebullience perfume, it's like delivering love. We all crave to be remembered and loved. I've continued Ebullience because that's exactly the lasting effect the perfume offers; Love and remembrance". Roberta's life reflects her epicurean tastes and pastimes. She and her family enjoy their time in the countryside around Venice and in the city of Chicago. She cherishes her show horses and takes pleasure from the wealth of aromas that surround her in nature. Roberta's powers of observation convinced her of the need to take on the legacy of Ebullience from its retiring guardian, Myron Hankin, when she noticed the striking and positive effect the fragrance had on every living creature that smelled it.

Derived from a rare blend of walnut woods, elaborate flowers and a principal flourish of violets from the south of France, Ebullience will linger from dusk until dawn on your skin, and forever in your memory bank. Fresh, pure and devastatingly sexy, this wonderfully feminine fragrance has known no equal since it first made its debut in 1978 taking America and Europe by storm. Its effect on women was instant: they loved it and couldn't get enough of it. Its effect on men was undeniable: they loved it on women and were attracted to those who wore it.

One of the oldest and longest privately owned boutique perfume companies in America, Ebullience is one of the original American luxury perfumes whose loyal following includes members of elite and royal circles through to discerning women (and men) on either side of the Atlantic.

In June of 2007, Ebullience perfume saw its new release at the prestigious Ball of Versailles in Paris hosted by its new envisioned owner and saviour, Roberta Balbo. Welcomed by distinguished audiences who have been captivated and enthralled by the magic it creates and the passion it elicits, Ebullience is truly one of America's crown jewels that will continue its legacy of excellence for years to come.

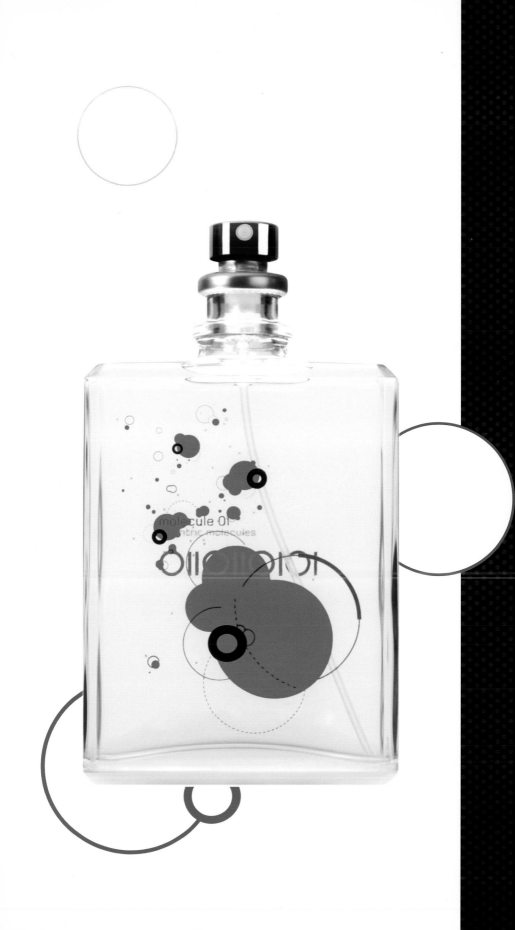

ESCENTRIC MOLECULES

MOLECULE 01

There are very few scents that truly have a 'wow' factor to them. Lots get a huge amount of publicity because of an expensive marketing campaign, but very few succeed in getting everyone talking about them simply because of the quality of the product. This is where Escentric Molecules have excelled, with Molecule 01, their star fragrance, attracting the kind of acclaim that other manufacturers can only dream about. Those who wear it find themselves in a secret society of understanding. Those who don't wear it become jealous at the wonderful and yet somehow elusive scent.

Molecule 01, the second scent created by Escentric Molecules, was designed by Berlin-based perfumer Geza Schoen as a provocative comment on the way perfumes are marketed and used today; in a sense, with its simultaneous understanding and rejection of the ethos of conventional scent, it's the perfect 21st century perfume. Geza came up with the idea of isolating a single scent ingredient and creating an entire fragrance around that. The result is innovative, trendsetting and groundbreaking.

Molecule 01 contains only Iso E Super, which is often used within other perfumes such as Christian Dior's Fahrenheit, to add a velvety note. It leads to a wonderfully subtle, lingering fragrance which manages to stay natural and clean yet sensual. It can linger on clothing for days, conjuring up a pleasant sensation for everyone who encounters it.

The intelligence and style behind Molecule 01 extends to every aspect of its distribution and promotion – although these two terms are too crude to describe the sophisticated and innovative way that the fragrance acquired its reputation. In partnership with two visionaries, branding genius Jeff Lounds of This Company and packaging gurus Me Company, Geza took an unconventional guerilla approach to marketing Molecule 01. They distributed bottles to choice individuals and sat back and watched as it became popular entirely via word of mouth. It boasts a huge celebrity fan base, including the likes of Elton John, Kate Moss and Mario Testino. But of course, they'd all be much too discreet to talk about it. The proof is entirely in the tell-tale scent.

Today, Molecule 01 remains sought after, simply through its inaccessibility. It is frequently sold out with constant waiting lists and people eagerly anticipating a new shipment. Demand vastly outstrips supply and, try as they might, Escentric Molecules cannot create as many as they need. It's unisex and remains a true 'talking-point' scent. Perhaps its unique appeal is best summed up by a keen admirer who said to Jeff and Geza, "This isn't your fragrance. This is my fragrance".

GROSSMITH

Imagine discovering your great-great-grandfather had established a successful English perfume house back in 1835. You bring the company back into family ownership and through meticulous research and lucky (fated?) coincidences you find yourself in possession of formulae books from the turn of the century. You discover that the company once commissioned its own range of Baccarat bottles. What started as a genealogy hobby has resulted in the revival of a world class brand!

This is exactly what happened to Simon Brooke. He found himself in this position— with an amazing opportunity in his hands—in mid-2007 and met Roja Dove by chance at the Haute Couture Exhibition at the V&A later that year. Since that meeting, with Roja's encouragement, Simon has worked tirelessly and systematically with his wife Amanda and an eminent team of advisors and suppliers—all the best in their respective fields. They have remastered and relaunched three of Grossmith's most popular scents: Hasu-no-Hana, Phul-Nana and Shem-el-Nessim in the UK in November 2009 and in the Middle East in February 2010.

The fragrances have been remastered as closely as possible to their original formulae using the finest natural materials irrespective of cost; thus maintaining Grossmith's ethos of exceptional quality underpinning arresting scents.

Hasu-no-Hana was created in 1888 to evoke the scent of the Japanese lotus lily and to coincide with the fascination with, what was then, a mysterious, closed country. It is a bright radiant floral composition with pronounced chypré and oriental facets on a woody dry, very sensual base.

Phul-Nana, originally created in 1891, encapsulated the essence of India (literally translated Phul-Nana means 'lovely flower' in Hindi). This fresh, sweet floral composition has aromatic fougere overtones on a soft, warm, woody base.

Shem-el-Nessim, which recognises the spring time festival celebrated on the Nile, was said, when it was created in 1906, to represent 'the scent of Araby'. Its warm, soft, powdery, floral aspect personifies the Edwardian era in which femininity was feted.

Simon's ancestors trained in Grasse and it is possible they came across members of the Guerlain family there. Shem-el-Nessim is said to resemble Guerlain's Apres l'Ondée (1906) and L'Heure Bleue (1912).

Grossmith was awarded Royal Warrants by Queen Alexandra and the Royal Courts of Spain and Greece – a wonderful accolade for its classic scents.

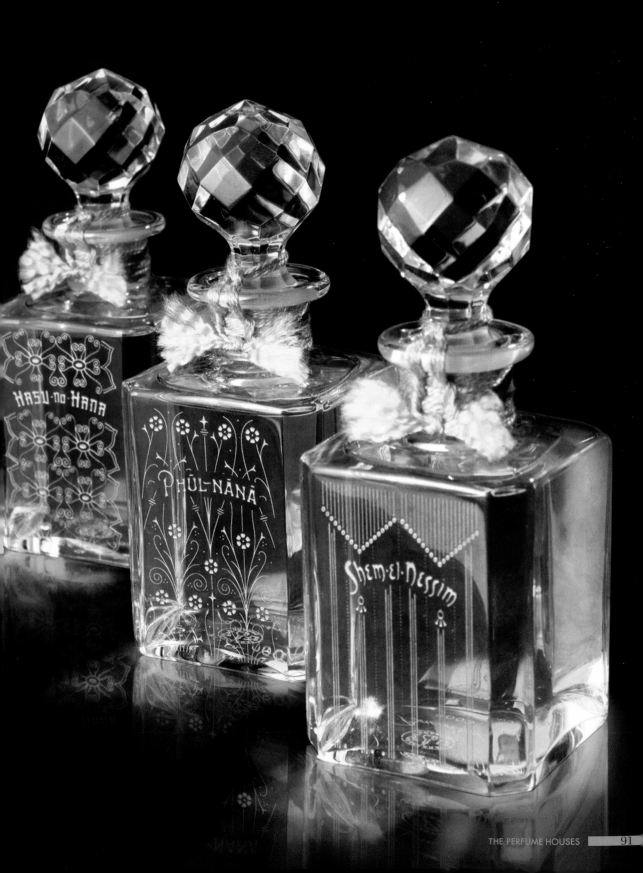

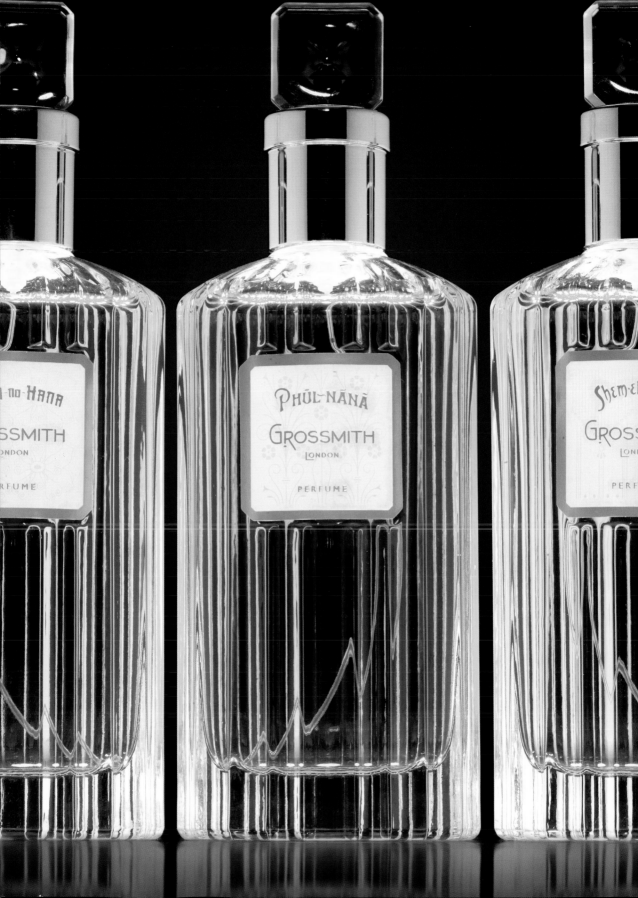

Roja Dove says "Grossmith played a significant part in the development of modern perfumery and occupied an important place as a fine English perfumery house at a time when English perfumery rivalled that of France. It has languished for many years and its revival is a welcome addition to the perfumery canon as Grossmith's scents have a wonderful complexity and quality which I believe is totally in tune with the current trend for authenticity, legitimacy, and individuality."

Grossmith's launch trio evokes a time when the English were enchanted by the idea of exotic, foreign places. Perfume wearers, then, could be transported by the simple application of a fragrance. Today's discerning perfume lover may be better travelled but will adore these classic fragrances for their beauty and heritage.

The Baccarat crystal flacon has been taken as the reference point for the design of the range. The Baccarat bottle's chamfered square profile is revisited in the presentation boxes, the signature overcaps, the labels of the perfume and eau de parfum as well as the perfume blotters. The original oval bottle shape has evolved into an elegant, distinctive reeded form. Grossmith's gorgeous faceted presentation boxes will add an air of luxury to any dressing table.

A special edition of newly blown Baccarat bottles has also been commissioned. Using the original 1919 mould it is decorated in pure gold in a contemporary interpretation of the original designs. A white lacquered box with dark blue lining, gold monogram and logo and a golden key perfectly complement the special concentrated perfume in its Baccarat flacon.

It is Simon and Amanda's aim to visit every store in which their perfume will be sold to meet and keep in touch with owners and staff and ensure purchasers know the fascinating story behind what they are buying. Thus ensuring that the perfumes remain exclusive, sold only in specialist perfumeries.

"I am overjoyed that a series of events, which began with an interest in family history and my discovery of the original formulae, has brought about the revival of the house of Grossmith and a new beginning for this classic brand. I am deeply proud of my ancestors' past achievements and feel privileged that, with Grossmith back in family ownership, I can continue the tradition of innovation and product development. We have some marvellous names and formulae to draw on and exciting plans for the future of Grossmith." – Simon Brooke, May 2010.

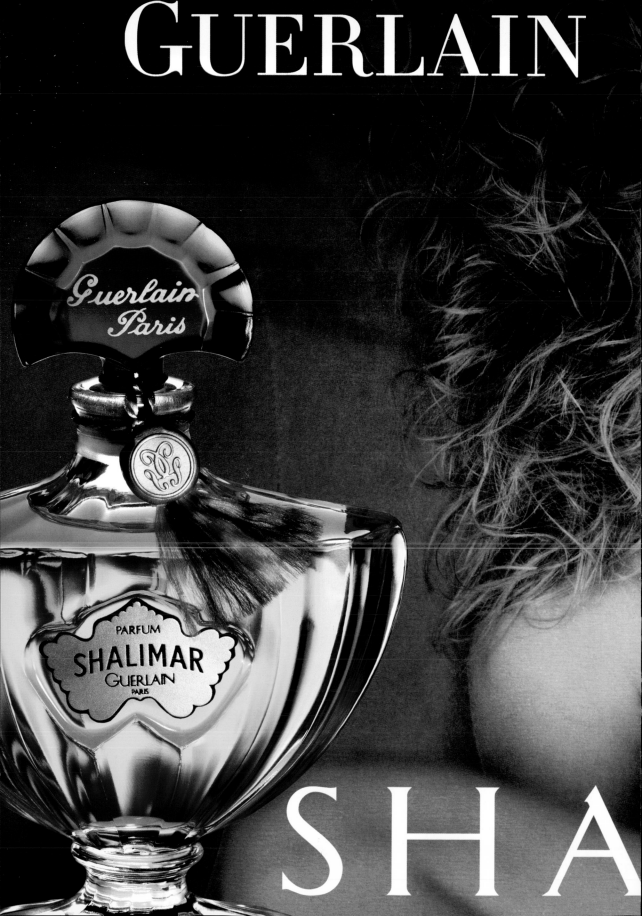

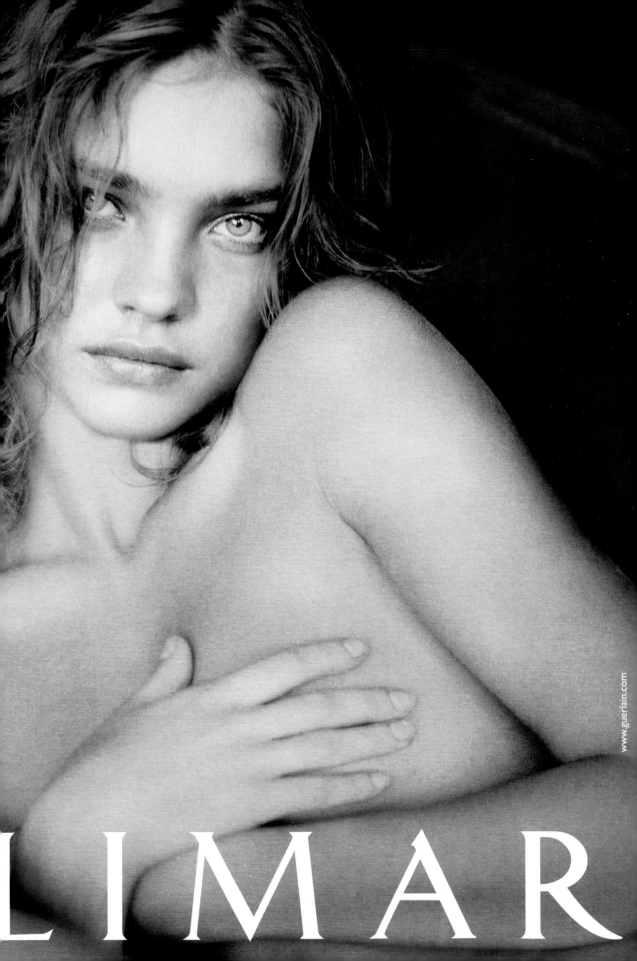

LIMAR

The House of Guerlain is one of the most well-established, influential and highly esteemed perfume houses of all time. Following in the footsteps of five generations of talented Guerlain perfumers and their exceptional creations, is the internationally successful perfumer Thierry Wasser. He was appointed as the first in-house perfumer for Guerlain outside of the family dynasty in June 2008. With his beautiful feminine fragrance, Idylle, and the wonderfully woody, aromatic Guerlain Homme, he has successfully transported Guerlain into a new fragrance era; one which bears all the hallmarks of the house's rich heritage and reputation for excellence, whilst embracing a contemporary new vision for the house.

Thierry Wasser & Jean – Paul Guerlain

It was Pierre-François-Pascal Guerlain who laid the foundations for the Guerlain house as its first perfumer. In 1828 he opened his boutique in Paris and was soon admired for his extraordinary fragrances. He was inspired by Empress Eugénie to exclusively design Eau de Cologne Impériale for her, prompting his appointment as her Official Supplier.

When Pierre-François-Pascal died in 1864, his eldest son Aimé took over as the firm's perfumer and revolutionised the face of Guerlain forever. In 1889 Aimé created Jicky, the first modern and groundbreaking fragrance to contain synthetic materials. Around this time, Aimé's teenage nephew Jacques started composing his own creations. His time as house perfumer was remarkable as he treated the world to Mouchoir de Monsieur in

1904; Après l'Ondée in 1906; L'Heure Bleue in 1912; Mitsouko in 1919; Shalimar in 1925 and Vol de Nuit in 1933. Shalimar was the first Oriental, noted for the use of the synthetic ethyl-vanillin that intensified Shalimar's redoubtable vanilla scent. The fragrance was the talk of the industry and was embraced by perfume lovers the world over.

Many of the Guerlain fragrances contained the legendary olfactory accord known as the Guerlinade. The Guerlinade is a complex construct known to be made up of bergamot, jasmine, Bulgarian rose, iris, tonka bean and vanilla, which underpins the fragrance. However, the exact proportions of these aforementioned notes vary according to the fragrance in which they feature (for example the quantities of vanilla are much higher in Shalimar than in l'Heure Bleue or Mitsouko) and these details remain resolutely guarded. The result is a Guerlain 'signature' that lends so many of the house's fragrances a unique quality.

Jacques worked well into his old age, devoting much of this time to training his 16 year-old grandson Jean-Paul, who then took over as his successor two years later in 1955. Jean-Paul's passion for perfection, for the meticulous research of materials from all corners of the world, made him a worthy successor. Indeed, the exclusive use of rare and precious materials such as ylang-ylang from the Comores Islands, Florentine iris or Indian tuberose is integral to the house of Guerlain and the inimitable magic of its fragrances. Jean-Paul's first solo scent creation in 1959, the elegantly crisp Vetiver echoed this. However his fragrances often paid homage to the women he loved or was moved by and the wonderful Chamade (1969); Nahema (1979) and Samsara (1989) are a true testament to them.

Since 2008, Thierry Wasser's devotion and loyalty to the values of the Guerlain house; to the unequalled quality of its fragrances and to future development, are a credit to the role he has inherited. His compositions with Guerlain bring a positive and modern influence to the house lineage and show his mastering of the language of Guerlain, keeping it vibrant and relevant. With many of the house fragrances surviving as classics to this day, Guerlain's roots run deep. Today Thierry Wasser is taking this extraordinary house to ever greater heights and will continue to captivate generations to come.

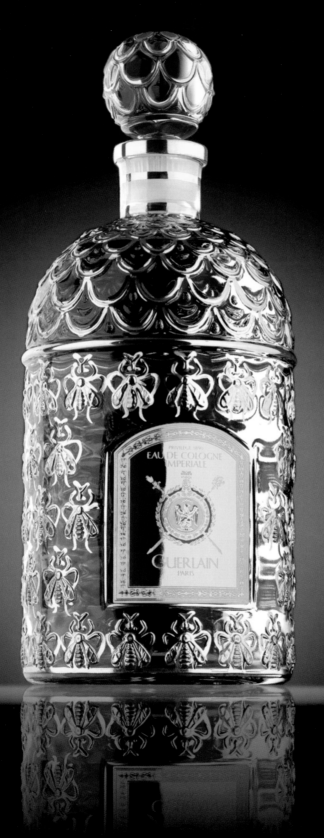

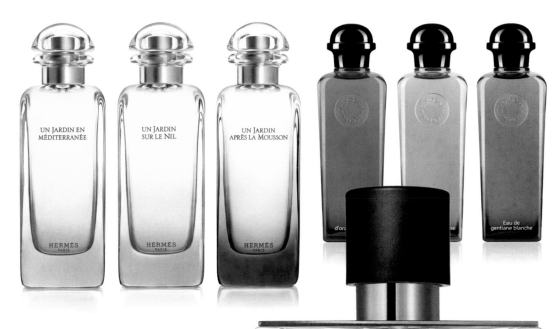

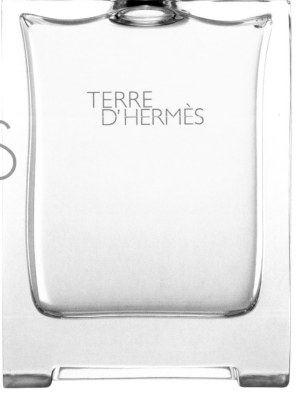

HERMÈS

One of the last remaining family owned businesses of its kind, Hermès is a splendid illustration of flawless craftsmanship – from the impeccable leather accessories that command year-long waiting lists, to the elegant fragrances that this house has been producing since 1951. Eau d'Hermès was the first creation, composed by the legendary perfumer Edmond Roudnitska in association with Émile Hermès. Originally conceived to describe the delicate scent of the iconic Hermès bag, the effect is seductive and beguiling, marrying fresh aromatics with rich and sensual civet. This singular and captivating composition has enthralled perfume enthusiasts ever since and paved the way for the house's future fragrances, notably the wonderfully feminine Calèche created by Guy Robert. Calèche celebrates floral aldehydic notes and is admired for its likeness to the feel of a silk Hermès scarf against a woman's skin. A little later in 1979, Eau d'Orange Verte delighted men and women with its combination of sparkling lemon, mandarin and orange; the dry down of leather and moss, however, made for an entirely different Cologne, full of character and distinction.

Hermès had made its unfaltering mark on the perfume world and the appointment of perfumer Jean-Claude Ellena in June 2004 seamlessly transported the house into a new and exciting era. Mr. Ellena's creative process and philosophy fitted perfectly with the house's own identity and high standing. His already impressive portfolio of fragrances composed for the likes of Cartier and Bulgari (to name but two), pointed towards a potential collaboration with Hermès. It was a perfect match and Mr. Ellena stated "in this great house, with its profound commitment to craftsmanship, I am realising a fantastic dream: living my passion with both creative rigour and complete freedom". It was in fact during his studies at the Givaudan School in Switzerland, that he discovered the work of Edmond Roudnitska and felt inspired and compelled to enter the perfume profession. His flair and passion is evident in all his creations: Un Jardin en Méditerranée, a sumptuous blend of sun drenched fig and Mediterranean citrus; Un Jardin sur le Nil, a journey to the Nile at Aswan with green mango, lotus, incense and sycamore wood; and Un Jardin après la Mousson which depicts the wonders of India. There's also the Hermessence collection, a series of fragrances exclusively created for selected Hermès boutiques that deliver the finest combinations of precious materials and essences for men and women.

Recently the internationally acclaimed Terre d'Hermès secured its ranking amongst the world's best-selling scents once more. This modern classic for men explores the elements of earth, air and water with layers of vegetal, woody and mineral notes. The depth and sensual tones are subtle, complex and instantly appeal yet the intimate character of Terre d'Hermès is the epitome of modern luxury.

Voyage d'Hermès, launched in 2010 is an infectious mix of genres; comforting yet energizing, familiar yet surprising, for both men and women this woody fresh and musky fragrance illustrates a journey. Jean-Claude Ellena wanted to create a perfume that people would smell and say, not: "It reminds me…" but: "It's calling to me."

Hermès has come to signify understated elegance and refinement: qualities which, when combined with the strength of vision that has taken the house into the new millennium, make for timeless and unequalled grace.

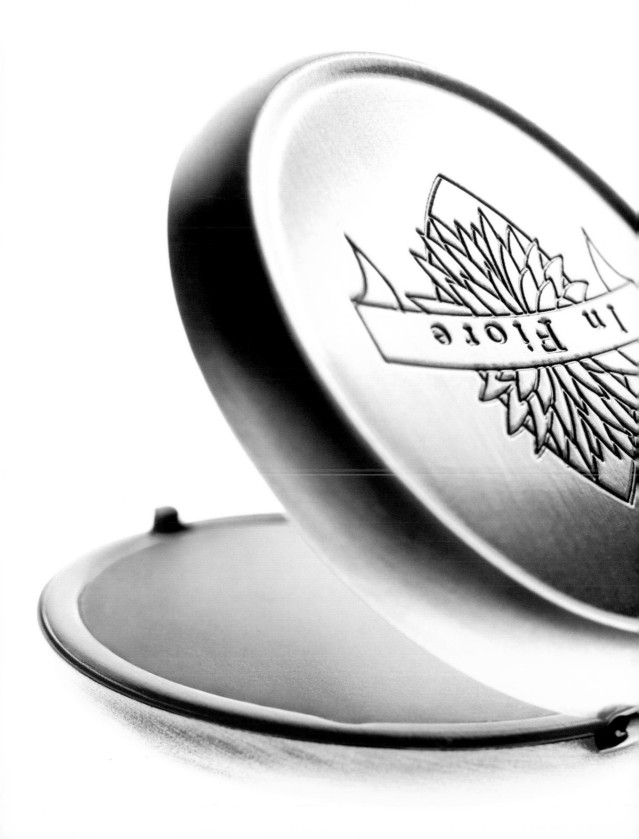

IN FIORE

In Fiore prides itself on offering a truly seductive experience for both skin and soul. Its distinctive beauty line combines the healing benefits of plants with the fragrant luxury of their scent. Exotic, decadent, fragile and precious, their properties are simultaneously gentle and powerful in their restorative abilities. Its proudest claim is that the innovative products can invigorate as much as they relax – a rare but powerful combination.

In Fiore had an auspicious beginning when Julie Elliott, a fashion veteran, was seduced by the opportunity to combine exceptional floral materials with fantastic health benefits, and was compelled to share this with others. In Fiore made its appearance in 1999 as the first skin care line to be blended with pure oils and expensive floral absolutes. The products hit the spot and acquired an instant and loyal following.

Inspired by old world apothecaries, Julie practices her craft with the dedication and the accumulated wisdom of centuries old tradition. She is not led by trends or the latest studies, only her innate affinity with scent and for blending, a passion that first began when she was young. Using simple, organic materials like wild biodynamically crafted essences and the finest absolutes, she has travelled the world in search of the most exotic materials – Bulgarian rose, Tunisian neroli, Indian jasmine... Her formulas illuminate nature's perfect simplicity and maximise its wondrous healing properties. Her intention is to let nature speak for itself. This minimalist approach shows that Julie's intention is to have an artist's vision as well as a craftsman's eye. It requires a real understanding of components: each flower's scent, character, profile, virtues. It's this intimate knowledge – the tropical hint of Indian rose, the femininity of jasmine – which makes In Fiore fragrances so nuanced and remarkable.

Julie Elliott's products include such items as Rose Noir body oil, which has gentle notes of Damascena rose and Assam oud to create a lingering and rich experience. Or Chamomile, a luxury pedicure balm that combines chamomile and lavender flower oils to regenerate skin cells, removing heat from the skin and reducing inflammation. It is this variety – the way in which her scented oils allow her to move from classic liquid to solid perfume and act as a balm on the skin – that keeps Julie at the cutting edge of creation.

In Fiore's power is impressive: invisible yet potent, able to summon the deepest of emotions and help us escape daily life. Each blend remains approachable and user friendly although its full story may be deeply complex. From the clean aesthetic of the smooth, elegant compact perfume balm to the alluring treatments and fragrances safely contained within, In Fiore will have you hooked. It feels gorgeously vintage yet its multi-usage is cleverly modern. As a pioneer in the scented cosmetics market, In Fiore embraces the spirit of invention and will thrive for generations to come as a forward thinking brand rooted in a legacy of tradition.

JEAN-CHARLES BROSSEAU

Jean-Charles Brosseau is a man of fashion with a keen sense of aesthetics that feature throughout all his creations. His style embodies pure refinement, classic and contemporary elegance and sophisticated craftsmanship.

As soon as he arrived on the scene his designs became an overnight sensation gracing the pages of Vogue, Glamour, Marie-Claire and Elle across the world. And shortly after he was inspired to create a perfume base to enhance his elegant fashion. Conjuring childhood memories of rice powder, Ombre Rose is a gorgeous, soft floral composition rich with Italian iris, honey, vanilla, peach and ylang-ylang. Encased in an octagonal bottle reminiscent of the 1920s – the overall effect perfectly complements the scent within frosted glass and a sober jewel-like top. None of the Jean-Charles Brosseau bottles bear any name, but they are instantly and visually identifiable. All the fragrances speak for themselves, as do his hats and fashion accessories, and it seems apt that the quote "The one fragrance that will make you forget all others", should be the only writing featured on the bottle for Ombre Rose.

The Americans immediately fell for the charms of this romantic scent, which was so different from the green apple and patchouli fragrances that were characteristic of the period. Bergdorf launched Ombre Rose in 1981 and gave it pride of place in their window displays – the first perfume to be granted this honour. International success soon followed and, at this point, the range expanded with hugely successful scented body lotions, shower gels, body creams and body powders.

The next Jean-Charles Brosseau fragrance marked a departure – an adventure – as it explored the solar floral fragrance family. Inspired by memories of beach holidays and far flung destinations, Ombre Bleue perfectly captured the scent of sea breeze, carnation, mimosa, vanilla and monoï oil. A winter pick-me-up like sunshine in a bottle, this fabulously evocative fragrance has seduced fragrance enthusiasts for years and has firmly placed Jean-Charles Brosseau amongst the world's finest perfumers.

In 2005 the delicate floral collection Fleur d'Ombre (which includes Ombre Bleue) reinforced his position and brought the brand right into the 21st century tapping into modern tastes with daring blends. Presented in individually coloured signature bottles it is difficult to choose between them as they're all so delicious. There's Violette-Menthe dusted with violet and blackcurrant like a walk in the woods or Jasmin-Lilas a spring breeze with green leaves, jasmine, lilac, nectarine and pineapple. Luxurious flowers are the star of Rose which blends that particular flower with jasmine and freesia making a perfect 'young' fragrance. In 2006 the much awaited men's Collection Homme celebrated masculine chic and individuality with the launch of Brun – laced with cumin and lapsang-souchong – and the equally stunning fragrances Atlas Cedar and Fruit de Bois. More recently, in the Fleurs d'Ombre collection, Bergamote – a citrus-floral blend with bergamot, jasmine and base notes of tonka bean and amber – is a sunny, delicate scent that fits like a glove. Jean-Charles Brosseau is a remarkable designer who appeals to generations of men and women and whose work will remain a reference for modern fragrance.

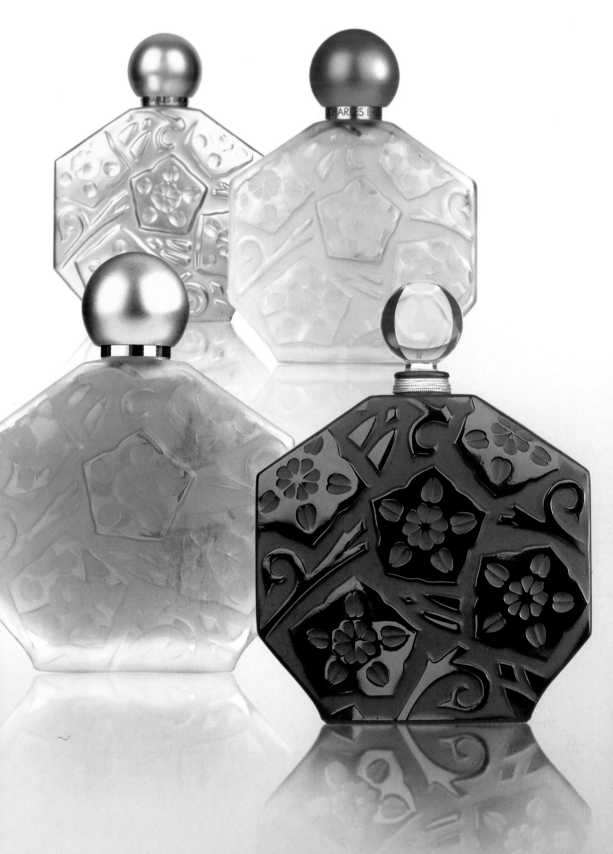

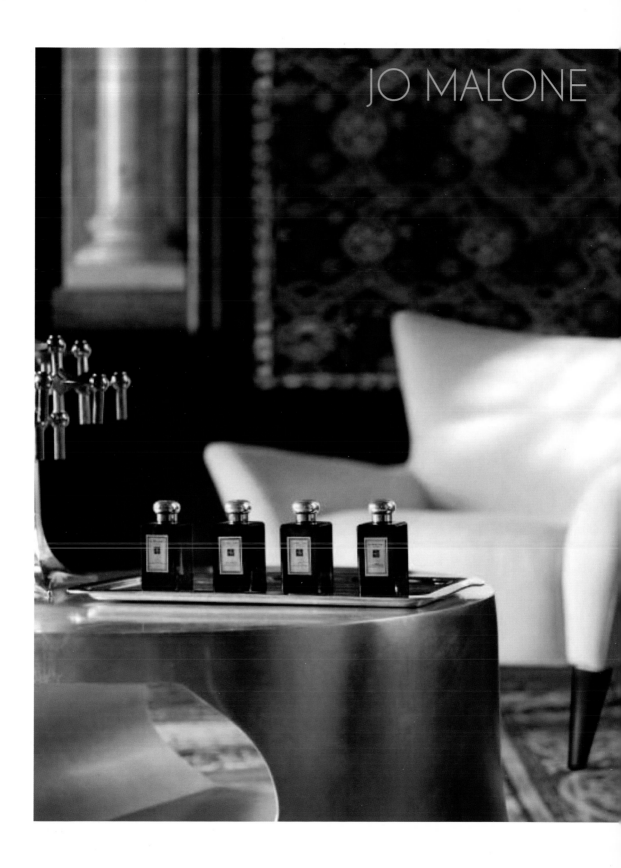

JO MALONE

Deeper. Richer. Yet manifestly fresher. While Jo Malone's new quartet of fragrances – Cologne Intense – honours some of Middle Eastern perfumery's most venerated ingredients, the collection simultaneously reframes and refines them with a luminous and utterly contemporary touch.

In Rose Water & Vanilla, the sweetly succulent aromas of a traditional Rose Mokhalat are given an unexpected edge with the bitter orange bite of neroli. The mysterious, hypnotic Oud & Bergamot radiates with an unanticipated clarity. Proving opposites attract, Iris & White Musk is a creation of beautifully controlled contrasts – the creamy, animalic nature of the musk note is fanned with the powdery airiness of precious iris root. While the union of opulent Amber & Patchouli harmonises happily thanks to a specially distilled patchouli essence that delivers a distinctly different, suede-like finish.

Each Cologne Intense plays with provocative dualities. Light and darkness. Depth and freshness. The old and the new. Simplicity and surprise. Each can either stand alone as a compelling statement of singular elegance or be layered with other Jo Malone colognes for endless bespoke effects. In this they reflect the Middle Eastern love of wearing a coalescence of scents and oils and also work beautifully with the Jo Malone philosophy of fragrance combining.

A sweeping arc of more than 20 fragrances – encompassing citrus, fruity and floral scents, right through to spicy and woody colognes – has been structured so that each fragrance can be layered with others in myriad ways. And with sumptuous bath products and body crèmes an intrinsic part of the artistic alchemy, it's an ethos that puts the wearer at the centre of the creative process.

It was Jo Malone herself who devised this direction more than two decades ago, opening her first boutique in Walton Street in 1994 and the flagship store in Sloane Street five years later. With a deep respect for the integrity of perfumery and an intuitive understanding of the genius of simplicity, she started to create fragrances that not only celebrated elegant restraint, but were also enlivened by a twist of the unconventional. In fact, the desire to pepper her first

citrus composition with fresh basil was considered so unorthodox it required a protracted pilgrimage to find a perfumer who would collaborate with her. Luckily, Lucien Piguet's interest was sufficiently piqued to help her create what is now a signature scent – Lime Basil & Mandarin. The coveted Home Candles and Living Colognes can be combined in similar ways; they form the basis of another intrinsic element in The World of Jo Malone – scent surround – born of the belief that the aromas in your home should be as inviting and expressive as the fragrance on your skin.

Visit any Jo Malone boutique in the 22 countries around the world and your perfumed purchase will be lovingly placed in the, now iconic, cream box nestled in rustling ink-black tissue and tied with a pristine black grosgrain bow – the hallmark of the Jo Malone art of gift giving. Both the continuity and evolution of this luxurious, intimate – and quintessentially British – brand lies with the Jo Malone Creative Studio, which still retains some of the original staff and is headed up by Dominic De Vetta who took on the role of Global General Manager in 2008. Appreciating the distinct DNA of the brand and committed to craftsmanship, it is De Vetta who personally invites prestigious perfumers to collaborate with the Creative Studio on all new projects.

For Cologne Intense, De Vetta enlisted the award-winning Christine Nagel. "Each of our fragrances is characterised by simplicity, transparency and a certain restraint and Christine shares our philosophy of simplicity as the epitome of elegance," he explains. Indeed, Nagel delights in creating fragrances in which no note is superfluous. "I like to focus on an ingredient and 'tame' and transform it." She says, "Cologne Intense is about embracing the beauty of another culture from a Jo Malone point of view." In so doing, Jo Malone explores a new olfactory direction – the fusion of richly evocative resonance with contemporary freshness, while at the same time, celebrates the timeless values at the very heart of perfume traditions.

Written by Jan Masters

L'ARTISAN PARFUMEUR

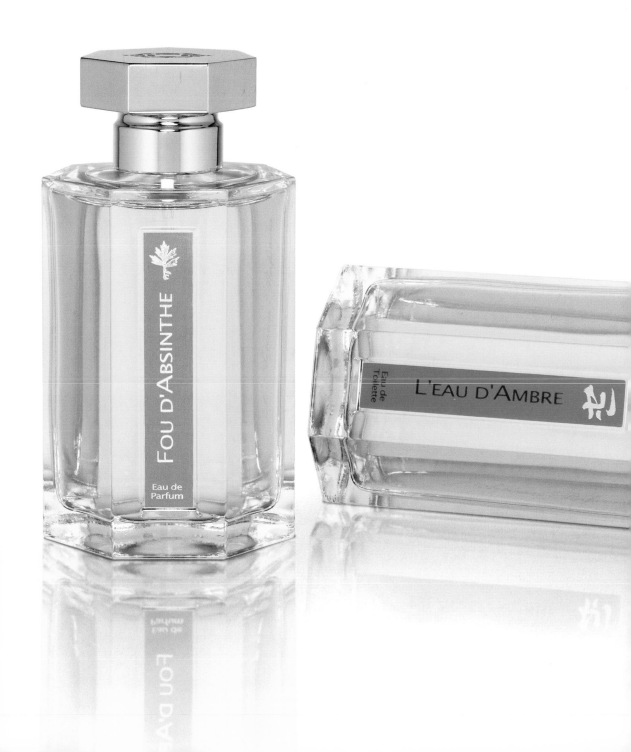

Since it was established in 1976 by French perfumer Jean Laporte, L'Artisan Parfumeur has successfully combined the traditional values of French perfumery with unusual and enchanting scented explorations. Perfume enthusiasts the world over have come to love this charming brand for its inspirational fragrances based on the wonders of nature and treasured memories. The magic of l'Artisan Parfumeur's universe is reflected in every little detail: elegant facetted bottles with weighty gold plated stoppers; distinctive box encasing coloured to suit the fragrance inside; and exceptionally welcoming boutiques. Many of the brand's eau de parfum and eau de toilette for men and women have achieved cult, if not classic, status. Premier Figuier created in 1994 was the first fragrance to use fig as its central theme and set a worldwide trend for fig based scents. Mûre et Musc based on juicy blackberry and soft musk is fresh and irresistible, launched in 1977 it remains the brand's star performer to this day. These interpretations of Mother Nature have paved the way for an impressive series of collaborations with master perfumers including Olivia Giacobetti, Bertrand Duchaufour, Michel Almairac, Jean-Claude Ellena, Evelyne Boulanger and Anne Flipo.

Romantics and adventurers alike can escape to exotic and imaginary destinations with the merest whiff of any one of the brand's fragrances. But most notable are those in the dedicated Voyages series that includes renditions of Bhutan in the wonderful spicy Dzongkha; Reunion Island in the deliciously nutty Bois Farine; the depths of Africa in the sweetly spicy Timbuktu; Cuba in the smooth Havana Vanille; and lately, the charms of the Middle East with the sensual Al Oudh. Al Oudh explores slightly darker aromas with its natural woods and rich leathery spices wrapped in oud, rose, candied dates and incense.

The brand is also known for its selection of exquisitely presented home fragrances, body products (soaps, shower gels and body lotions) to accompany certain fragrances, and hand crafted scented objects that make coveted gifts and keepsakes. Creative home sprays, candles, terracotta pomanders and silk flowers that delicately scent and adorn wardrobes and rooms. In addition to these olfactory wonders, l'Artisan Parfumeur is keen to bring innovative ideas to its discerning followers. A novel patented product called Chez Moi, unique to l'Artisan Parfumeur is an ingenuous system that allies technology, design and beauty diffusing scent into the home through a battery powered box; fully portable a perfumed bead is placed into the box and the selected scent is distributed with one touch of a finger. Two new skin care ranges, Jatamansi and Côte d'Amour based on organic ingredients have added further breadth to the collection along with limited edition fragrances and a bespoke service – Mon Numéro – which allows to select your own secret, numbered fragrance formula, exclusive to you.

Intimate fragrances, a personalised service, precious materials and a creative approach to nature's beneficial and scented properties – these are all qualities which have defined l'Artisan Parfumeur's luxurious and poetic character and which will continue to enthrall us for years to come.

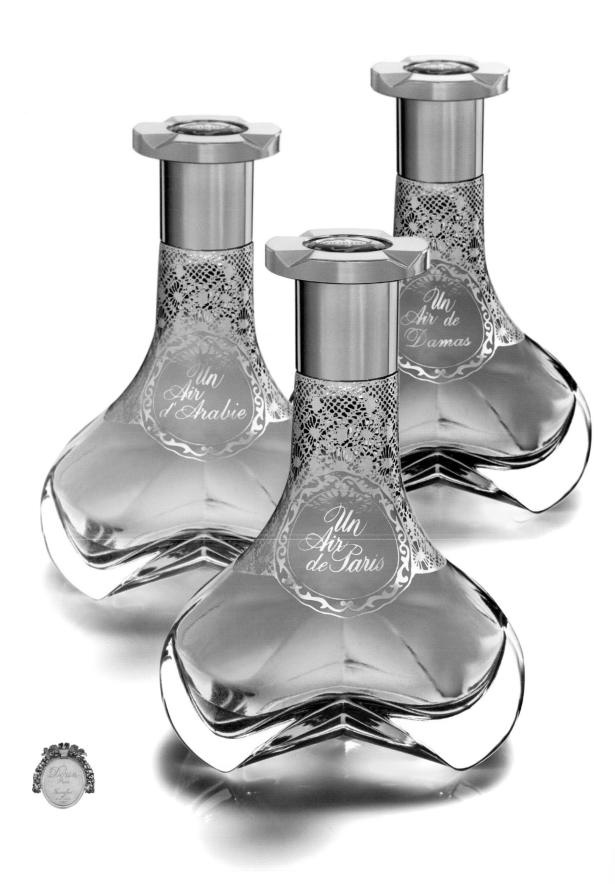

MAISON DORIN

Maison Dorin was born in the latter part of the Ancien Régime in the 18th century at a time when art and beauty reigned supreme. The house was considered a symbol and guarantor of feminine beauty. Perfume made its debut at the Royal Court during the Regency period when people started using powders, blush and creams, but it was only through the influence of Marie-Antoinette (1755-1793) that perfume became more sophisticated. The Maison Dorin afforded such research and attention to detail when creating textures and scents that it became the subject of much admiration amongst aristocrats and nobility, not least when in 1780 it became official purveyor to the Royal Court of Versailles.

Towards the end of Louis XVI's reign, the house boutique on the Rue Grenier Saint-Lazare in Paris had become the place to be for any self-respecting noble. The founder of the store was Marguerite Montansier, a celebrated actress at the time whose experience in luxury, cosmetics and female aspirations was instrumental. Indeed the skill and artistry behind these unique creations was remarkable. Some cosmetic and scented products achieved masterpiece status and can still be admired today at the Musée Carnavalet in Paris and the Municipal Art and History Museum in Colombes. From these noble origins came the art of the Maison Dorin.

The perfume industry underwent a transformation with the advent of science under the Empire (1804-1815). With this the Maison Dorin strode triumphantly ahead modernising all its working methods. No expense was spared on creating the largest and best equipped laboratories in Paris, thus successfully outwitting all its competition for decades to come.

The Universal Exhibitions in Paris (between 1839 and 1889) opened the floodgates to the foreign luxury market. The Maison Dorin secured the enviable role of exporting to England, Russia, Spain and America, and its excellent reputation was sealed. There were outstanding successes in Moscow (1891), Chicago (1893), Brussels (1897), a Gold Medal in Paris (1900), the list goes on. The taste for good perfume and cosmetics was at its peak and the Maison Dorin built enormous shops and factories producing scientifically advanced products that continued to dominate the world market.

Fast forward to the 28th of January 1998 – the Maison Dorin was rightfully given a new lease of life thanks to Bashar and Imane Nasri, allowing this prestigious house the chance to shine again. The original inspiration and influences intrinsic to the excellence of the brand have been re-introduced with great aplomb and vision. In 1998, they created the Candle Light collection in memory of Princess Diana, the proceeds of which went entirely to charities supporting handicapped children. Un Air de Paris, the wonderful classic scent created in 1896, was re-launched in 2007 bringing it contemporary success followed by fruity, floral and spicy versions in 2008. Oriental fragrance enthusiasts are indulged with the floral collection Un Air de Damas (including the fragrances Rose de Damas; Jasmin; Tubéreuse and Fullah) and the sensual collection Un Air d'Arabie (including the fragrances Oud; Ambre; Musc and Rose de Taïf).

With a gradual return to core values in perfume making and a need to regain a sense of personality in fragrance, the Maison Dorin revival couldn't have come at a more poignant time. One thing's for sure – this is one perfume house that won't let the past (and future) of excellence and quality out of its sights.

Some of the prize–winning and pioneering Maison Dorin scented cosmetics:

a. Marie Antoinette lipstick case

b. Gold plated duo powder compact

c. Un Air de Paris powder box

d. Lady's powder box

e. Gentlemen's powder box

f. Nail strengthener

a

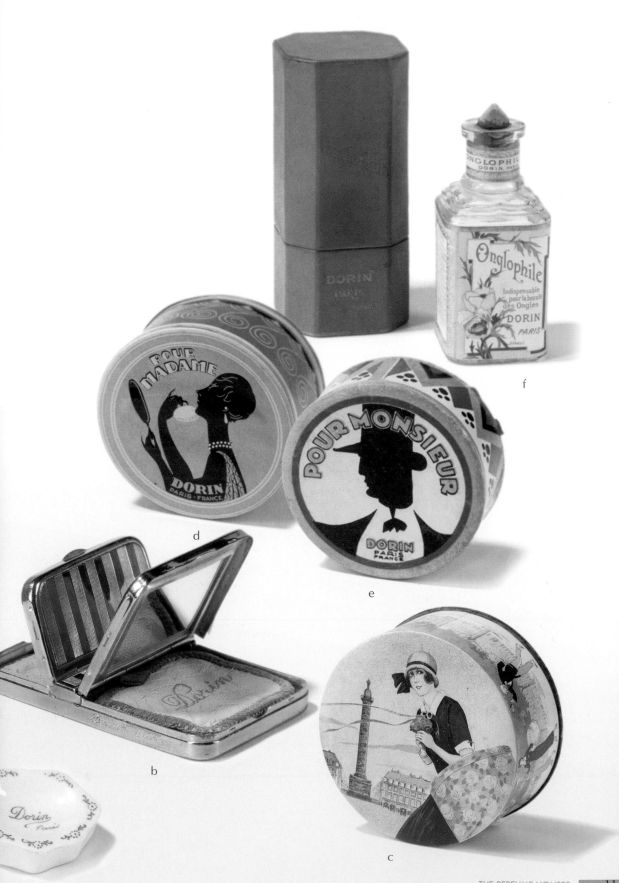

f

d

e

b

c

MILLER HARRIS

British luxury fragrance house Miller Harris perfectly expresses perfumer Lyn Harris' irreverent and eclectic style, combining the finest raw materials with delicate artistry and instinct. Time spent playing as a child amongst the scented flowers, herbs and vegetables in her grandparents' garden in Scotland left a vivid impression on her olfactory memory. When Lyn took her first job in the world of fragrance those memories began to resurface. The wealth of materials and expertise at her fingertips triggered a fascination with the link between smell and emotions. Having studied the science of natural materials, she went on to complete classical training and the art of natural fragrance creation in Paris and then Grasse. It made perfect sense that later on she would establish her own company, Miller Harris, as a means of expressing her passion for perfumery. Lyn's philosophy is to combine simple, beautiful raw materials with flair and invention.

The result is an intelligent mix of tradition, heritage and innovation present in all her fragrances and products. It's also echoed in the iconic packaging that features an 18th century print of botanical plants set against a background of vivid colours, as well as the distinctive style of her stand-alone boutiques. Never one for complacency, Lyn Harris constantly surprises her audience with new ideas – fragrant teas and olive oils, beautifully printed lifestyle goods and textiles.

As the UK's first independent perfumer, Lyn pioneered bespoke perfumery over 20 years ago at a point when such a service was unheard of in London. Today, she is one of the most respected bespoke perfumers in the world and she has created private blends for a wide array of high profile clients including members of royal families and A-list celebrities. Lyn's talent as a bespoke perfumer also led to the launch of L'Air de Rien, created for and with iconic actress and singer Jane Birkin. The principles behind Lyn's bespoke business inspired her to launch the Miller Harris brand as a vehicle to express her own vision and creativity.

The brand boasts a rich selection of fragrances to explore and a good place to start would be the vibrant, spirit lifting, Citron Citron; like a celebration of Mediterranean sunshine with lemon, orange and lime, warmed by a touch of basil, cedar and moss. For those seeking a little contrast, Figue Amère inspired by the bitter, ripe green figs found on the coast of Ibiza, is a curious and delicious blend of fleshy fig and salty sea breeze.

With a 10th anniversary to celebrate, 2010 sees the launch of four anniversary editions of her original classic fragrances revisiting the formulas to create a collection of Eaux Parfumées. A fitting tribute to these much-loved fragrances adding new dimension to them for the future. The good news now is that Miller Harris is set to grow and spread the brand's creative spirit further afield in Asia, Australia, the Middle East and The Levant.

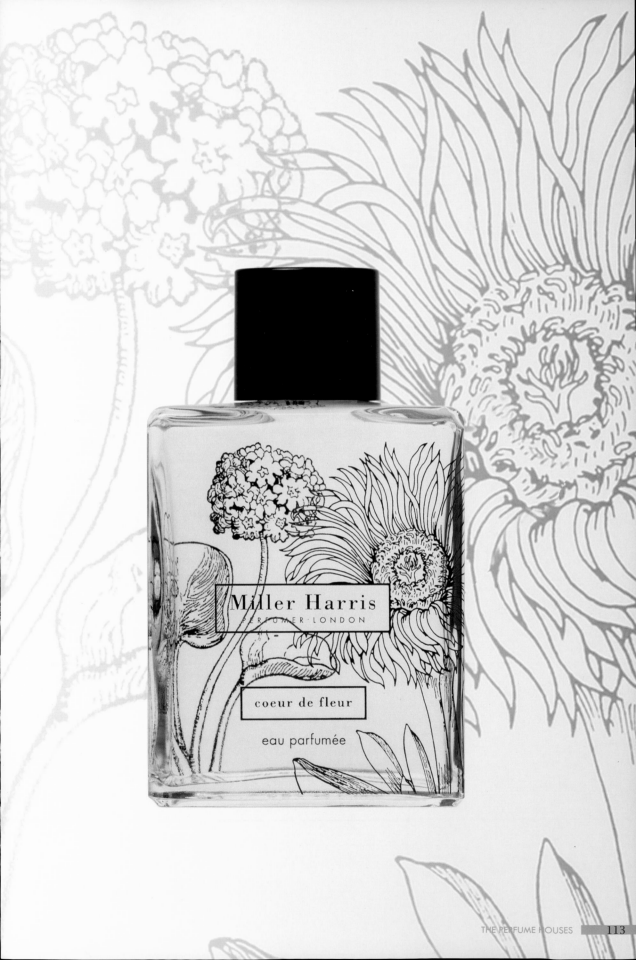

NARCISO RODRIGUEZ

New Jersey born fashion designer Narciso Rodriguez embodies passion, style and integrity – qualities integral to his personality and work. He began his career at Donna Karan and Calvin Klein. His motivation and success soon saw him take the role of design director at Cerruti and Loewe in Europe. He subsequently received global recognition – not least for the beautiful bias-cut sheath wedding dress he designed for Carolyn Bessette when she married John F Kennedy Jr. From Salma Hayek to Sarah Jessica Parker and Oprah Winfrey, his glamorous clients pledge loyalty to a designer whose creations embrace the feminine form with elegance, grace and respect. His fundamental understanding of women is enriched by the wealth of inspiration he draws from colours, textures and his New York environment – such as

architectural symmetry in buildings or works of art. Idea are carefully recorded in a montage of words and visuals resulting in the stunning creations we see on the catwalk

His perfume creations are a natural extension of his creativity, and when his first fragrance, For Her, made its entrance in 2003 it was welcomed with great acclaim throughout the fragrance world. Purity, elegance, precision and sensuality lend distinction to the addictive scent. It was created in collaboration with two eminent perfumers and celebrates the many facets of Mr Rodriguez' favourite note – musk.

Musk beats at the heart of For Her, gently revealing osmanthus floral notes, sensual amber and delicate vetiver, with patchouli woody notes beneath. As the musk unfolds, For Her amplifies in a round of note reminiscent of the enveloping softness of a downy cloud. It breathes sensuality and remains mysterious long after its initail appeal.

It came as no surprise that the subsequent fragrance creations from Narciso Rodriguez – For Him in 2007 and then Essence in 2009 – were also greeted with great praise and excitement. With Essence, he developed a pure and luminous construct of musk, embodying supreme sensuality and ultimate femininity. One touch of this all enveloping scent and women fall for its radian aura – rich with rose petals, powdery iris and seductive hints of amber. All of these wonderfully blended notes are wrapped in the inimitable veil of modern musks. It's hard to resist the attractiveness of this extraordinary material in all its guises.

Narciso Rodriguez brings intelligence, insight and his native Latin sensuality to his clothes and fragrances associating American ready-to-wear fashion with European *haute couture*. His universe is one where traditional elegance sits comfortably alongside innovation and modernity. He has become part of a generation of young American fashion designers whose creations honour the past and define the future of classic elegance. A powerful talent to possess as it will always be in fashion.

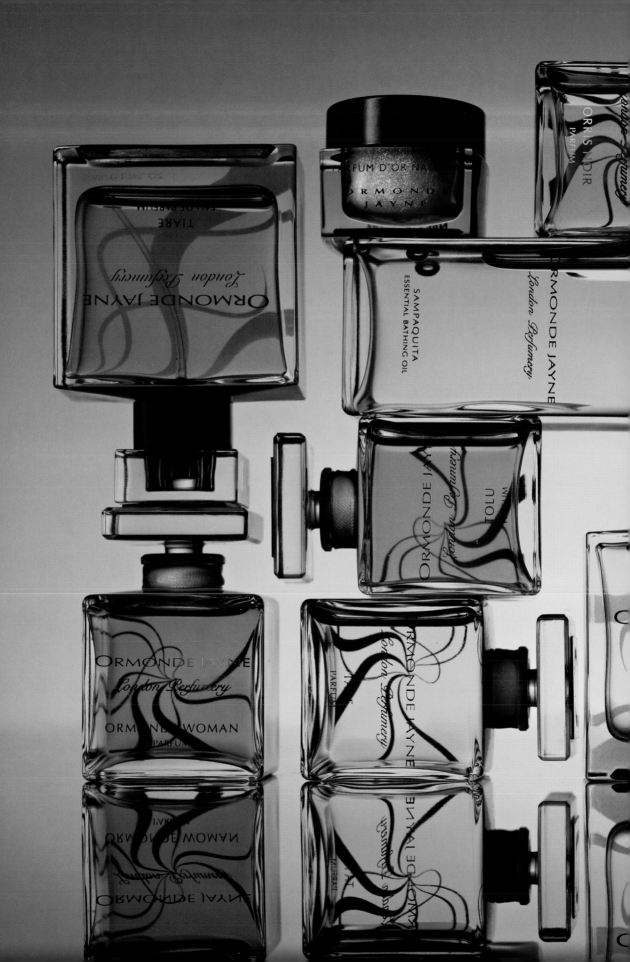

ORMONDE JAYNE

Ormonde Jayne is a company devoted to the pursuit of beauty and elegance, imbued with the highest quality of materials and presentation. The aim is pure and simple – the production of beautiful and sophisticated scents using the finest materials available, including some that are rarely smelled in today's perfume industry. Their avowed aim is 'to be at the cutting edge of creativity, defying convention in the world of scent', something that they have certainly achieved.

The company was founded by Linda Pilkington, who is a hands-on creator and very much involved in the selection process of the raw materials. She first became involved in perfume by making scented candles, and her creative impulses soon found a fuller rein. It is Linda's tireless commitment to producing flawless quality that has seen her travel widely; researching and sourcing ingredients from locations as disparate as the Horn of Africa to the Laos border in Thailand. Linda has always expressed her desire to combine elements that she feels can epitomise true elegance. She combines the wonders of English craftsmanship and the art of French perfumery with natural oriental blends.

No job is too small – be it the development of packaging, spending time with customers looking for their signature scent in her flagship boutique in the Royal Arcade on Old Bond Street; or masterminding the company's expansion into the Middle East. Her innovative online store has also allowed perfume lovers worldwide to dip into her world and reward her with their loyalty. Some of the most respected and admired actors, artists and perfume experts in the world proudly swear allegiance to her fragrances. Her painstaking attention to detail includes beautifully engraved bottles and gorgeous gold-flecked solid perfumes. Every experience and aspect of her creations is designed to appeal to even the most demanding perfumer lover.

Perhaps most refreshing, however, is Linda's modesty and generosity which is reflected in her fragrances. Her eponymous first scent, Ormonde Woman, swiftly moved into the best selling lists for alternative perfumery with its lusciously bitter notes of black hemlock absolute – a note seldom used to such glorious effect. Other highlights include: Tolu, which is perfect for men and women – a sensual oriental perfume with wonderfully dry juniper berry, orchid and Moroccan rose; Isfarkand – a vibrant fragrance suffused with mandarin and bergamot oil, and the signature fragrance, Ormonde Man a beautiful oud based scent. It was no surprise that Luca Turin, a leading perfume scientist and biophysicist, awarded her five stars in his seminal book: Perfumes: The A-Z Guide, an endorsement of her work and career.

Ormonde Jayne's distinguishing features are the ability to create balance between refinement, delicacy of touch and constant innovation. There can be little doubt that Linda's endless inspiration and her striving for perfection is inextricably linked to the beauty and success of her brand and a British perfume Renaissance.

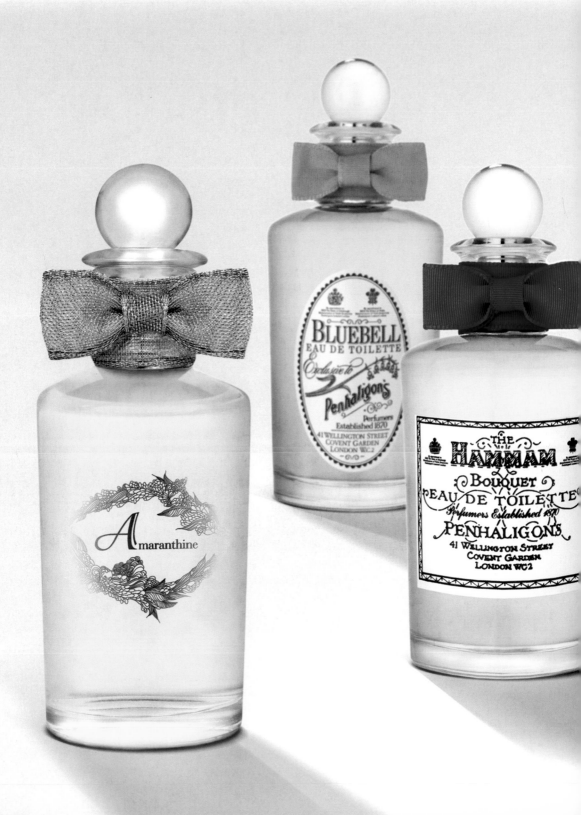

PENHALIGON'S

Penhaligon's has clearly understood what perfume means to us mere mortals. They believe that perfume is liquid emotion. It's capable of unlocking memories; of stopping us in our tracks and transporting us to another place and time where the scented trail we leave behind us lives on eternally in the minds and memories of others. These recollections are triggered by a dusting of iris, a whisper of clove, a burst of juicy nectarine, a lick of vanilla.

You could say that Penhaligon's forte is the quintessentially British style with which it approaches the exotic. Ever since William Penhaligon was first compelled to create Hammam Bouquet in 1872, his spirit has lived on – drawing inspiration from colourful dreams and wild imagination. Penhaligon's first scent was inspired by the steam and sulphurous aromas of the Turkish baths that adjoined his barber's shop on Jermyn Street. Its daring sensuality was way ahead of its time. Turkish rose, wood, lightened with jasmine – not what you'd expect in a man's fragrance but it works so beautifully, it continues to bewitch legions of men (and women) to this day.

In 1902 came the groundbreaking Blenheim Bouquet. Breaking away from the heavy scents in fashion at that time, Blenheim Bouquet's blend of citrus and camphor-like freshness took the fragrance world by storm.

Penhaligon's embraces change and continues to work with innovative master perfumers. Bertrand Duchaufour's appointment in 2009 was a stroke of genius. Respected for his bold, inventive work and sense of fun; perfume lovers are in for a treat. Elegant tradition and modernity have rarely been so well matched. The scents are still made in England using the finest rarest ingredients – from hand-squeezed bergamot to jasmine at twice the price of gold. The signature fragrance bottle has kept to William's original design: clear glass with a distinctive ribbon-wrapped top.

The fragrance collection is as varied as it is beautiful. There are stunning soliflores like Lily of the Valley; rich orientals like Malabah and crisp fougères like English Fern. More recently Anthology, a series of archive scents dating back to 1927 and reinterpreted for the 21st century, has delighted purists and modernists alike. The collection is so divine you won't know where to start.

In the autumn of 2009, Amaranthine, a new feminine fragrance was launched. Created by Bertrand Duchaufour, this corrupted floral oriental is seductive and intoxicating. Its success is testament to the dynamic team driving the brand; it is with passion and spirit that Penhaligon's strides triumphantly into the 21st century. Times may change, trends may ebb and flow but the spirit of Penhaligon's is definitely here to stay.

PRO FVMVM ROMA

Pro Fvmvm Roma occupies a unique corner of the 'niche' fragrance world. When the Durante family left the small Italian town of Sant' Elena Sannita in the early 1950s, their aim was to create something lasting and important that would stand the test of time and leave a lasting legacy. The family had a tradition of skilled craftsmanship and they soon opened their first shop with the intent of producing luxurious handmade scented products such as soaps and hair lotions. In no time at all the family business became an enormous success. In 1996, Giuseppe, Luciano, Felice and Maria Durante decided to develop their achievements further and created their own fragrance range, Pro Fvmvm Roma.

To describe Pro Fvmvm Roma as mere fragrance is too simple to do the range full justice. With over 20 fragrances to its name, it is a unique olfactory concept where scent is seen as part of the inner self rather than an external signature. With a rich family background, the Durantes have always understood how perfume can become an extension of our soul, of our dreams, and Pro Fvmvm Roma embraces these dreams in each story it tells.

Every fragrance is imbued with its own particular set of emotions and associations; each setting a seductive scene for the wearer, plunging them into another world. Take Acqua di Sale, which literally means 'salty water' – close your eyes and as you breathe in the delicate salty/sweet notes of sun scorched myrtle, cedarwood and seaweed, imagine yourself by the sea: the breeze blowing through your hair, exhilarated by the energizing particles in the air, clouds rolling through the sky, your skin lightly covered with a dusting of salt and sand, your mind drifting contentedly.

Then there's Dulcis in Fundo laced with sparkling Sicilian citrus and voluptuous vanilla. It conjures up memories of childhood happiness and sweets you once loved, wrapped within a grown up scent. It's fruity yet powdery, sweet yet subtle and it possesses an enveloping and velvety quality that is wonderfully comforting.

Ichnusa smells of the Mediterranean forest where the sun beats down as the crickets sing their mesmerising song, dry pine needles litter the ground and there is a promisingly luscious scent of fresh, ripe figs. Taking notes of vetiver and smoked birch, it beautifully evokes glorious memories of holidays in Greece, Italy and the south of France.

The beauty of these scents is their ability to effortlessly transport you to places you may never have been but yet places that feel strangely familiar. They open a window into the recesses of the memory and touch a deeply personal chord; like slipping into a tailor-made suit or dress, or reliving a beautiful dream that is long forgotten. Pro Fvmvm Roma believes that "sometimes, a scent is more evocative than a photo or an image. It is the trigger for an explosion of sensation, emotion, desire, atmosphere and uncontrollable *déjà vu*". And it's true to say that once you've witnessed this first hand, you can do little else but surrender to its fragrant charms.

ACQVA VIVA

PROFVMVM ROMA

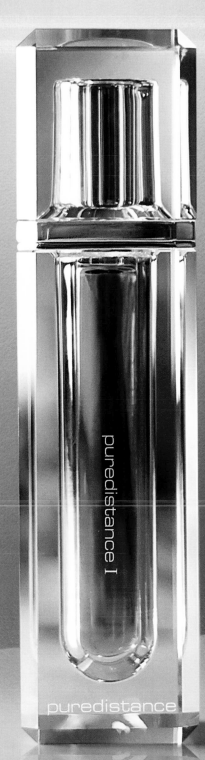

PUREDISTANCE

If PUREDISTANCE had to define itself by a simple motto, it would be 'understated elegance'. This is the guiding factor behind all of its innovations and initiatives, supported by its charismatic founder Jan Ewoud Vos. He comments that "all my life I have been fascinated by beauty in its most natural form… PUREDISTANCE is all about beauty. Pure Beauty". It took Jan Ewoud seven years to fulfill his long cherished dream – to create a concept of purity and timeless beauty – as he toiled away in a renovated church in the small town of Groningen in The Netherlands.

PUREDISTANCE – and specifically the fragrance PUREDISTANCE1 – came about through a meeting between Jan Ewoud and Master Perfumer Annie Buzantian. As fate would have it, Annie was introduced to Jan Ewoud's concept and was stunned to find that his idea perfectly matched her own; each realised that the other had unwittingly been inspired by the same image found in a magazine.

Since its launch, PUREDISTANCE1 has attracted a great deal of acclaim from perfume critics for its ingeniously balanced signature. It contains fresh tangerine blossom complemented by magnolia, jasmine, rose wardia, mimosa and lingering touches of amber, white musk and vetiver. The result is a beguiling contrast of cool and warm notes that keeps you guessing as they develop on the skin.

Presentation is crucial as it echoes the purity of the fragrance. The fragrance is presented in various forms. Most notably the Swarovski crystal column – each one individually number engraved on the base and in the cap; and the Black Crystal column, finished in gold or polished steel. The concept of a perfume spray contained inside a pure crystal column was originally envisaged by the acclaimed designer Sander Sinot, whose reputation for sublime simplicity inspired Jan Ewoud to create something unique and quintessentially PUREDISTANCE.

As the perfume is exclusive and original, so the retailer must be. The PUREDISTANCE Perfume Lounge in Vienna, designed by Philipp Metternich, a renowned architectural lighting specialist – is deliberately located in a stylish and iconic city. This flagship store has been designed to feel like you're walking into a five-star hotel lounge with stylish black and gold décor. It's intended as a shrine to the fragrance in which people can relax. Other stores that carry this luxurious brand are equally select and Jan Ewoud's next dream could mean a second lounge opening in the city of Paris; a perfect backdrop for beautiful design pieces to set off the fragrance collection as it grows. The company constantly thrives in an atmosphere of innovation and progress, never resting on its considerable achievements. As Jan Ewoud says, "I don't know where PUREDISTANCE will take me, or where I will take PUREDISTANCE, but I feel the journey is worth all the energy we put in; so we move on and try to enjoy this voyage as much as possible!"

fracas
DE
ROBERT
PIGUET
PARIS-FRANCE
bandit
DE
ROBERT
PIGUET
PARIS-FRANCE
bandit
DE
ROBERT
PIGUET
PARIS-FRANCE
fracas
DE
ROBERT
PIGUET
PARIS-FRANCE

Robert Piguet's name has epitomised classic and elegant fragrances since the 1940s. He was born in Switzerland in 1901 and soon moved to Paris, where he carved an illustrious career inspiring leading couturiers such as Redfern and Poiret. As his career developed, Piguet was considered to have made two indelible contributions, one to fashion and one to fragrance. Pierre Balmain and Hubert Givenchy trained at the hands of this fashion master as did Christian Dior who was quoted as saying "Robert Piguet taught me the virtues of simplicity through which true elegance must come". His other important gift was to the world of fragrance when his perfumes, such as Bandit, Fracas and Baghari, caused ripples of excitement. His fragrances reflected his values of 'good taste, true luxury, a horror of the commonplace and an innate sense of seduction'.

ROBERT PIGUET

Following his untimely death in 1953, the fragrances fell into obsolescence. Thankfully, several decades later they were revived by Fashion Fragrances & Cosmetics Ltd, which had the vision to revisit and re-introduce the legendary and unique fragrances to a new audience. They maintained the same bold attributes and high level of quality that Piguet had originally demanded in his scent.

Fracas – for many, the jewel in the crown of the collection – is an intoxicating combination of tuberose, gardenia and orange blossom. It was created for Robert Piguet by Germaine Cellier, one of the most highly respected female noses of all time. Fracas extended the boundaries of sensuality in the floral family – both shocking and compelling in its intensity. A cult secret, Fracas has become an industry icon and was inducted into the FiFi Hall of Fame as well as frequently featuring on celebrities and eminent luminaries' wish lists.

Bandit, Piguet's first fragrance created in 1944 is an intense blend of exotic leather, wood, spices and moss. One of Piguet's more androgynous scents, it presented a new and darker twist to the chypré family. It was a groundbreaker at the time

of its launch – models dressed as bank robbers sporting pistols sashayed down the catwalk and dramatically smashed bottles of Bandit on the floor displaying rebellion in true Bandit style.

Further beautiful scents followed with Visa in 1945 and Baghari in 1950. Visa has been fabulously re-orchestrated to blend modern radiance and retro glamour in an explosion of peach, pear, bergamot, rose and patchouli. Baghari's subtle floral and aldehydic softness is as relevant today as ever. As is Cravache; originally launched in 1963, this masculine fragrance was inspired by Piguet's love for horse riding in the countryside with invigorating yet sophisticated notes of aromatic citrus, lavender and wood notes.

Futur, Robert Piguet's romantic green floral woody fragrance originally launched in the 1960s, is the latest gem to be revealed to our modern audience. It fuses citrus notes, romantic flowers and rich woods. This fragrance is for those who choose to break with tradition and stand out in the crowd. If you take time to discover each of Robert Piguet's scents slowly and with thought, you'll be rewarded with a lifelong companion to suit every occasion in the most impeccable of style.

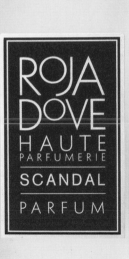

ROJA DOVE

As the most quoted fragrance expert in the world, Roja Dove's wisdom and passion bring the world of scent to life. He is a historian and a storyteller but above all he is the maestro of fragrance, the world's sole 'Professeur de Parfums'. He produces exceptional fragrances for exceptional people – whether private individuals, luxurious houses, global corporations, or international organisations – his style, creativity, quality and imagination resonate throughout his work.

After almost two decades of professional experience with Guerlain, Roja's journey into bespoke scents echoed his own inimitable style. It began at a charity event at Christie's Auction House in London after which success was inevitable. Boasting an exclusive clientele, Roja's bespoke fragrances are the definition of Haute Parfumerie, the olfactory equivalent of *haute couture*. How fitting then that each bespoke treasure should be housed in a Baccarat crystal flacon and composed with the finest, most precious raw materials in the world. Will Roja divulge his client list? 'No,' he smiles, because you know he knows, that you know who they may be. Discretion is the key.

Until today, only Roja's private international clients have been able to reserve one-on-one appointment time and enjoy that elusive "*je ne sais quoi*" that comes with the privilege of a bespoke fragrance. Luckily now, however, appointments are available with Roja himself or with the members of his highly trained team at the Roja Dove Haute Parfumerie, where you're expertly guided towards your signature fragrance, be it bespoke or semi-bespoke according to your wishes.

A haven of tranquility and refinement on the fifth floor of Harrods, The Roja Dove Haute Parfumerie offers the most exclusive fragrance brands, carefully selected by Roja for their quality, innovation and directional approach. This selection, in addition to the unique 'Odour Profiling' bespoke service (masterminded by Roja) and Roja's own Trilogy make for an extraordinary experience and a truly unique perfumery.

The Roja Dove Trilogy was crafted by Roja with the same passion, artistic flair and love as his bespoke fragrances. Celebrating the art of perfume mastery, each was created according to the methods used during the golden age of fragrance: without financial constraint or compromise, and without a marketing brief in sight. The result is a trilogy comprising a fragrance from each of the classic olfactory families: Scandal (a sumptuous floral), Unspoken (a smouldering chypré) and Enslaved (a soft, sensual oriental). "These are fragrances as precious as the great masterpieces once were; natural, complex, luxurious, but truly modern, interpreting as they do, the desire for real quality, real artistry, and real individuality." Roja Dove.

his most acclaimed fragrances and indeed his life. For Serge Lutens, Morocco was a crucial destination, which led to a wonderful romance with perfume. "During my first trip to Marrakech, in 1968, I had an epiphany when I found a piece of delightfully fragrant cedar in a small wood-worker's at the souk. It so overwhelmed me that I told myself I had to make a perfume from it. Then I totally forgot about it, until one day…"

SERGE LUTENS

The eventual result of this fragrant cedar was Féminité du Bois, in 1990. Serge Lutens was asked by Shiseido to create a line of original fragrances, which he refers to as "one of the most difficult things in my life". The intention was to "create a perfume that was different from all the perfumes in the world: a woman's fragrance made from cedar… In perfumery cedar had only ever been used in tiny quantities and mostly in men's fragrances." Serge succeeded admirably.

His scents are rich, layered, sensual and never predictable. They belong to a universe where gender isn't limited to stereotype and cannot be defined by any cliché. Scents such as Arabie, Fleurs d'Oranger and Daim Blond are complex and equally striking on men and women. His other creations include: Ambre Sultan, a softly resinous ode to amber that weaves through coriander, bay and oregano unfurling to reveal a sensual and lingering base; Arabie, imbued with the richness of exotic spices and fruits; Fleurs d'Oranger, that wraps you in its sweet-scented petals; and Daim Blond which balances soft white suede with bitter sweet apricot, powdery iris and heliotrope. Every fragrance boasts a very distinct 'personality' that envelops the wearer whilst respecting their individuality.

The name Serge Lutens has become synonymous with rarity and mystery in the world of fragrance. His creations are sought out by the most discerning and knowledgeable perfume lovers, and each new release is anticipated with excitement. This is not a reception offered to many perfumers, but then Serge Lutens is no ordinary perfumer.

Serge Lutens began his career as a stylist who was especially known for the daring and contemporary looks he created. He gained a real insight into beauty and the feminine form. After working as a photographer and make-up artist at Vogue in Paris, Serge Lutens enjoyed success at Dior. He continued, however, to seek out new inspirations which led to a chance 'meeting' with a boat that happened to be sailing to Morocco. The ensuing adventure was to influence and mold

Serge Lutens will always be French first, even though, he has adopted Morocco as his home, and it – in turn – has adopted him! It is Marrakech in particular that offers a source of endless inspiration for the perfumer who says, "you cannot be passive about fragrances in Marrakech, you are literally inside them – it's like a constant olfactory education." That, surely, is the secret of Serge Lutens' enviable success.

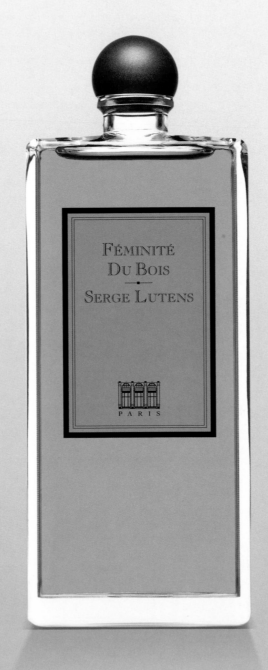

TEO CABANEL

Téo Cabanel has a fascinating history. Few houses make themselves great once; even fewer manage to do it twice. But there is little orthodox or conventional about Téo Cabanel, which prides itself on offering individual and outstanding artistry with all the style and forward looking creativity that might be expected from this great house. Originally founded in Boufarik in 1893 by a French doctor and chemist, Téo Cabanel has always produced flawless quality with delicate colognes, *extraits de mouchoirs* (handkerchief scent) and recently, solid perfume jewel like compact casing.

Caroline Ilacqua, the current president, was tied to the brand by fate, her family ties – her godmother was Cabanel's daughter – and enormous flair and vision. It is no exaggeration to say that her passion and vitality have turned the company around and brought this century old house into the 21st century, with its 150 formulae and historical

wealth. Having inherited the company at a young age in 2003, Caroline initially had no inkling that this would become her calling – she had already embarked on a career in advertising. However, upon meeting and joining forces with the inspirational perfumer Jean-François Latty, it became clear that she was destined to follow in the footsteps of her godmother.

The appointment of Jean-François represented a major coup for Caroline, as Mr. Latty is nothing short of a legendary figure. Having trained at the Roure Perfume Institute in Grasse, he then went on to work for Roure in 1970 followed by IFF and then, in 1987, Takasago, creating classics such as Givenchy III, Eau Dynamisante and Jazz YSL to name a few. The Cabanel heritage and its portfolio were so impressive that he had no hesitation in embarking upon a perfume Renaissance.

Amongst this beautiful collection is Oha – like walking through a dew drenched garden at dawn suffused with rose and jasmine. Then there's Julia – luscious and full bodied with blackcurrant, raspberry, violet and hyacinth. Or Alahine – a devastating and bewitching oriental, marrying ylang-ylang, jasmine and patchouli with vanilla and tree resins and Early Roses due to be launched in 2010.

Caroline has taken the company on a clear and exciting new journey. Hand in hand with her mentor and inspiration, Jean-François, she has developed new fragrances that combine richness and subtlety. Their style is true to the great French perfume tradition- the *Grande Parfumerie Française* – respecting its heritage whilst embracing innovation. Téo Cabanel enthusiasts can look forward to a new generation of luxury perfumery celebrating past and future fragrance creations with ingenuity and flawless elegance.

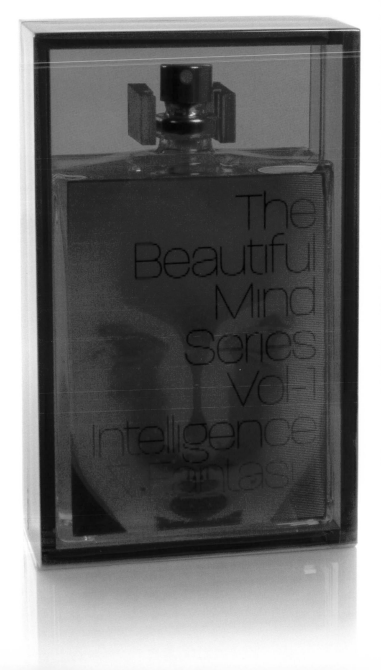
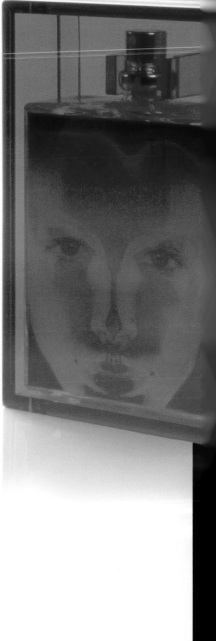

THE BEAUTIFUL MIND

The launch of The Beautiful Mind fragrance series marks an unprecedented collaboration between a well-known nose, a renowned graphic design company and an intellectual prodigy.

They are, respectively, Berlin-based Geza Schoen, Me Company in London and Christiane Stenger who, in her early teens, became a Grandmaster of Memory and the Junior World Memory Champion at the World Memory Championships. She subsequently won the competition two more times.

Schoen is well-known – some might say notorious – for the contrary positions he takes on fragrance industry conventions. That's how he came up with the cult sensation Molecule 01 (and its partner Escentric 01) which has become with its global army of fans as the anti-fragrance. Schoen found himself increasingly rankled by the flood-tide of celebrity fragrances attached to people who were famous for no other reason than that they were famous. He was more interested in celebrating the truly special skill of a woman with a scent. It was around this time he came across a magazine article about Stenger, now 22 and a political science student in Munich. Several months later she came to Berlin and the duo spent the month of July 2007 working together on what would eventually become The Beautiful Mind.

"It was so exciting to get an insight into something which is so hidden." Stenger recalls. "Geza has so much to tell – about fragrance, about the sense of smell and I learned so much. It was all over much too soon." It was a learning curve for Schoen too. "Memory is infinite," he says, "nothing touches it like our sense of smell. So it was amazing to watch Christiane use her incredible memory skills while we were working with the raw materials." It was this 'gift of nature' as he calls it, that Schoen set out to

The goal was a scent that would appeal to head and heart by connecting the mobility of the mind with the depth of memory. "An ode to summer and its memories", is Schoen's description. "A refreshing sparkle followed by tropical flowers, luscious woods and musk." Top notes include magnolia bud, bergamot, mandarin, schinus molle and freesia. The heart is composed of osmanthus, rose oil, hedione and, most critically, notes of tiare absolute extracted from a rare and expensive Tahitian flower. These floral absolutes give the scent a wonderful richness. The base of the fragrance is cedar, musk, sandalwood and cashmeran. Think of the way your mind edits the past into a series of vivid sense impressions.

Me Company's packaging is equally evocative. A transparent red box contains the bottle which is wrapped in a lenticular foil depicting Stenger's face morphing into abstraction. It's a complex, mesmerizing effect which compels consideration of the concept behind the fragrance. "The red reflects our life force, blood," explains Schoen, "and the movement of the foil is intended to evoke the flow of axons in our brain while we're thinking."

"It's spectacular." Stenger adds, "It reflects exactly what we wanted to express with the fragrance. The best thing is when you can see the eyes just for a moment. It's a reminder that we all should keep our brains moving."

A fragrance that celebrates the life of the mind with a lush appeal to the senses may seem a little paradoxical on the surface, but that in itself is perfectly in keeping with Geza Schoen's ethos. "Besides," he declares, "The Beautiful Mind is meant to remind us that a smart woman is a sexy woman."

THE HOUSE OF LUBIN

Pierre-François Lubin, one of the greatest perfume makers of the modern era, was born in 1774, the year which ended the reign of Louis XV. He died in 1853, shortly after the coronation of Napoleon III. From the Ancien Régime through to the beginnings of the Industrial Revolution, Pierre-François Lubin made a huge contribution to perfumery. He could be described as the first modern perfumer.

After his apprenticeship at Tombarelli's, a perfume master based in Grasse, Lubin left for Paris in 1790 to complete his training under Jean-Louis Fargeon, who was then still serving as the official perfumer to Marie-Antoinette. Everyday the Queen wore an eau de toilette with the scent of roses, which she loved most, and Fargeon captured this fragrance with much talent.

A Royal Tribute: Au Bouquet de Roses
Lubin began distilling his own compositions and in 1798 he opened his first boutique – *Au Bouquet de Roses* – a discreet tribute to the Queen, who met a tragic fate. His subtle blends and exotic fragrances soon made him popular with the first dandies who were known as *Les Incroyables* (the Incredible), while their extravagant and beautiful companions were referred to as *Les Merveilleuses* (the Marvellous).

When the Bourbon dynasty returned to power in 1815, Lubin claimed his title as the 'holder of beauty secrets of the French court', the legacy left by Fargeon. But even before that, under the reign of Napoleon I, Empress Joséphine already had the young and talented perfumer supply her scent. And Napoleon's sister, Pauline Bonaparte, (later to become Princess Borghese), even lent her name to one of Lubin's perfumes. Thanks to this illustrious patronage, Lubin was soon to become the favourite perfumer of the 19th century European Royal courts. In 1821, he became the official supplier to George IV, King of England, as well as to the Tsar Alexander I of Russia in 1823. During the reign of the last Queen of France, Maria Amalia who came to the throne in 1830, The House of Lubin finally obtained its title as the 'official perfumer of the French royal court.'

In 1844, The House of Lubin came into the hands of Félix Prot, who was considered by the founder as his natural successor and spiritual inheritor. Félix Prot built Europe's first modern perfume factory in Cannes which opened in 1873. Félix Prot's son Paul took over Lubin in 1885. A true visionary, speaking fluent English and German, he travelled the world and built a worldwide network, setting the basis for a truly international organisation. His sons Marcel and Pierre, who had joined the firm in 1911 and 1912, took the helm of the company in the early 1920s.

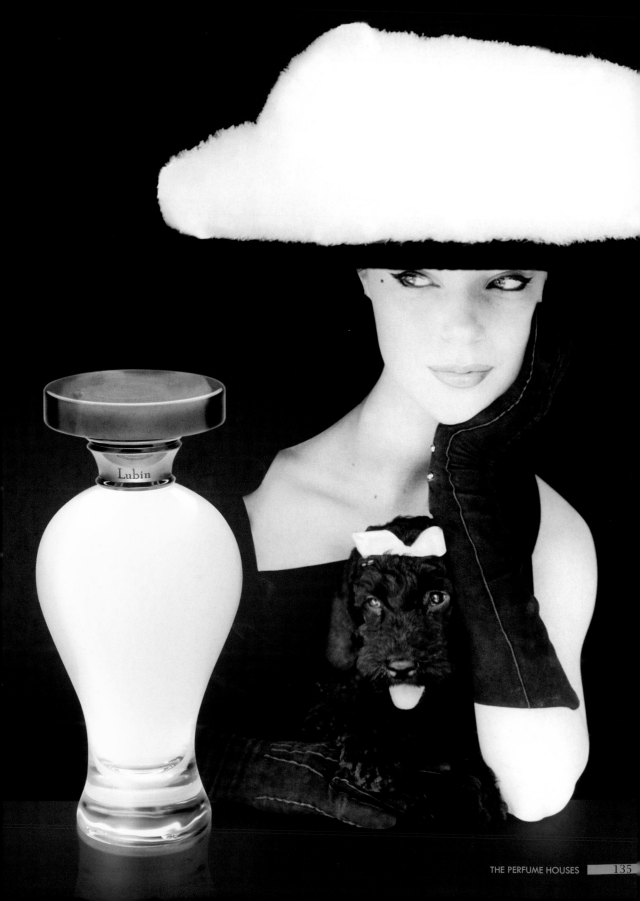

Villiers sur Orge 17 8bre   an 1808.

Le Secrétaire des Commandemens de S. A. Imp.
la Princesse PAULINE, Princesse BORGHÈSE,
Duchesse de GUASTALLA, Membre du Corps-Législatif,

Je vous préviens, Monsieur, que Son
altesse impériale, vous autorise à prendre le titre
de son Marchand parfumeur; La présente
Lettre vous tiendra Lieu de brevet.

agréez Monsieur mes salutations cordiales

Mr Lubin Marchand Parfumeur.

The Scent of New Territories

From then on, the company extended its global reach. Lubin perfumes were available the world over and were a symbol of French elegance for ladies of international society. New fragrances were launched in the 1920s and 1930s. Their bottles were created by masters such as Julien Viard and Maurice Depinoix. Luxury crystal editions were produced by Baccarat. Their success owed as much to the originality of the scents as to their outstanding bottles. Lubin's greatest commercial success, however, was in America. It began in the 1830s, when The House of Lubin set up local premises in New York, New Orleans and St. Louis. The scents were favoured by local artistocratic families, particularly in the Old South where plantations were owned by families of French descent.

The Great Depression in 1929 hit Lubin very badly. Fortunately, Nuit de Longchamp, a timeless scent created in 1937, became a particular favourite with the American public, thus saving the company from bankrupcy. Pierre's son Paul Prot and his cousin André joined Lubin at war's end in 1945. The new team launched Daïmo in 1947, followed by Gin Fizz in 1955. The latter a creation of perfumer Henri Giboulet, paid tribute to one of the most beautiful women of the time, Grace Kelly, future Princess of Monaco. Gin Fizz had tremendous success and allowed Lubin to once again set its mark on the world, despite growing competition from new perfumes entering the market by couturiers.

Lubin entered a period of slow but steady decline in the 1970s, despite the successful launches of L'Eau Neuve in 1968, and L de Lubin in 1975. The house was taken over by Mülhens in 1984, who relaunched it on a global scale in 1987 and it was finally sold in 2004 to a consortium of French perfume specialists. They managed to save the historical perfume house.

A sculptor of world renown, Serge Mansau and perfume genius Olivia Giacobetti were already working in parallel on the bottle and fragrance for the newest version of Idole. This perfume, launched in October 2005, was to be Lubin's first creation of the 21st century. It allowed Lubin to re-establish its status as an exceptional perfume house of great acclaim.

The Lubin archives, safeguarded by both the Mülhens company and some of the Prot family members, helped revive Lubin's unmatched olfactory style and provide the missing details to forgotten formulae. At the beginning of the 21st century, The House of Lubin has now regained all the glory of its former past. It continues to immortalise its founder's ideals, creating perfumes of the highest creativity and quality that will enchant generations to come.

TOM FORD

You could say that Tom Ford has the Midas touch. From revolutionising the fortunes of Gucci to dressing men and women in his own iconic designs; from directing an award-winning film to creating beautiful fragrances, his eye for detail and nose for success have hit the spot with a skill that others can only dream of.

The Tom Ford Private Blend Collection has brought glamour and sophistication back to artisanal fragrances. The designer himself has described this fragrance collection as "my own scent laboratory; it's where I have the ability to create very special, original fragrances that are unconstrained by the conventions of mainstream scent-making. Private Blend is designed with the true fragrance connoisseur in mind."

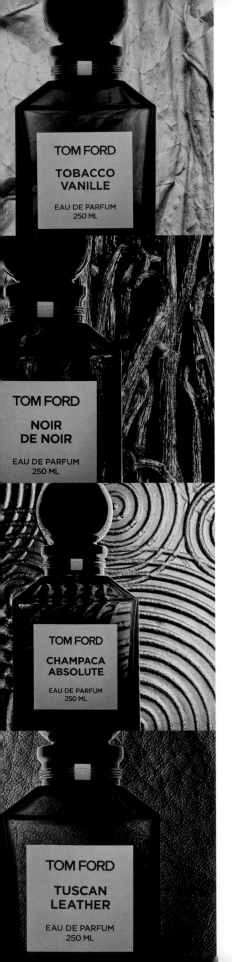

TOM FORD

TOBACCO
VANILLE

EAU DE PARFUM
250 ML

TOM FORD

NOIR
DE NOIR

EAU DE PARFUM
250 ML

TOM FORD

CHAMPACA
ABSOLUTE

EAU DE PARFUM
250 ML

TOM FORD

TUSCAN
LEATHER

EAU DE PARFUM
250 ML

Packaged in a single bottle design, each of the fragrances explores the most compelling and precious perfume notes such as amber, tobacco, black violet, leather, gardenia and oud wood. As these top notes develop, they're then joined and warmed by middle and base notes that round and complete each fragrance to mesmerising effect. The bottle, inspired by the dark brown glass of the perfumers' apothecary bottles used in their work rooms, is stylish, sober and suited to men or women – none of the fragrances have been categorized by gender. The 50ml spray bottle is weighty in the hand with a simple gold label and clean lines that resemble a sleek chess piece. The 250ml decanter, adorned with the same label, is carved with skillful craftsmanship and is a beautiful ornament in its own right. The details add the finishing touches of luxury: hand blown glass, crimped cord ties around the bottle neck and the textured box encasing. Each scent creates a distinctive aura that in turn will surprise, invigorate and bewitch its wearer.

You'll be spoilt for choice when you discover each fragrance in the collection is as breath-taking as the next. Amber Absolute celebrates the purest form of amber with rich African incense, labdanum, woods and vanilla bean. Noir de Noir is a fabulously dark and sophisticated chypré laced with saffron, black rose, black truffle and earthy touches of tree moss. Italian Cypress is sartorially inspired and was created especially for the Tom Ford store in Milan, it's as exhilarating as a breath of fresh air; all resinous sap, pine needles and natural woods that whisk you away to the Italian hills. The floral composition, Champaca Absolute, is gourmand and suffused with mouth watering jasmine, broom, orchid and cognac. All the joy of a naughty dessert without any of the guilt.

These are just a few of the 16 fragrances in the collection so far and it's well worth dipping into each scent and taking time to discover them all. The chances are that you'll fall in love with them over and over again, and the hardest question you'll have to answer will be, which one to choose first?

VAN CLEEF & ARPELS

Van Cleef & Arpels has an impeccable reputation as a world class jeweller. Over the past three and a half decades this reputation has extended to a range of flawlessly elegant fragrances and they have firmly secured their place amongst the most admired fragrance designers of recent times. The family business was founded in 1906 and it was one of the first luxury European companies to move across the Atlantic to America in 1939. The jewellery collection acquired a faithful fan base of legendary figures, such as Marlene Dietrich and Grace Kelly, so it was no surprise when the house expanded into the world of fragrance.

Of the many sublime fragrances that Van Cleef & Arpels have created, one of the most iconic is First, created by the supremely talented perfumer Jean-Claude Ellena in 1976. First was launched when Jacques Arpels resolved to offer his female customers a fragrance to equal the beauty of his jewellery. First like a gloriously sensual bouquet of flowers swiftly shot into the bestselling fragrance list. It has notes of hyacinth, orchid, amber and the superbly animalistic civet. The dual aspects of sophistication and simplicity captured in First continue to enchant women year after year and the fragrance initiated the trend for intensely rich florals that shaped the late 1970s and early 1980s.

Van Cleef, the second iconic scent from Van Cleef & Arpels launched in 1994. Crisp, green and wonderfully powdery, Van Cleef offered welcome respite from the glut of 'ozonic' or translucent scents flooding the market at that time. Perfume trends come and go, but Van Cleef became an olfactory classic with its seductive blend of earthy galbanum, vibrant orange blossom and spicy carnation. It is as sharp and smart as a perfectly fashioned gem, and certainly as timeless.

Feerie was the next women's fragrance to delight, bringing enchantment to the world of luxury fragrance with a faceted astral blue gem topped with a delicate magical fairy. The fragrance notes hint at sophisticated opulence with blackcurrant buds, Bulgarian rose absolute, Egyptian jasmine, vanilla and Florentine iris, finally shimmering with the scent of the most precious woods, including majestic Haitian vetiver.

In recent years Van Cleef & Arpels have made waves in the perfume industry again with their Collection Extraordinaire – six rare and luxurious scents for men and women created from the most precious raw materials. The collection has a bespoke feel that suggests exclusivity and each scent boasts an individual and well respected perfumer.

The most recent addition to the women's fragrances of the Van Cleef & Arpels family is Oriens. The shimmering faceted tourmaline sphere atop the bottle celebrates a notable ring created by a fine jeweller who was inspired by the house's oriental cultural heritage. Oriens continues the era of the fragrance-jewellery combination at the heart of the Van Cleef & Arpels brand. The olfactory journey reinforces the influence of the orient: it is peppered with fleshy red fruit notes, such as raspberry and blackcurrant, amid transparent petals of jasmine and patchouli with praline finally developing in the base to give a sensual and captivating aura.

Van Cleef & Arpels is dedicated to unparalleled quality in both its use of the finest raw materials and its most talented and individual perfumers. The link between the jewellery and fragrance of the house is distinguished at every turn with prevailing dedication to luxury. For these reasons we look forward to future generations of spectacular olfactory gems from Van Cleef & Arpels.

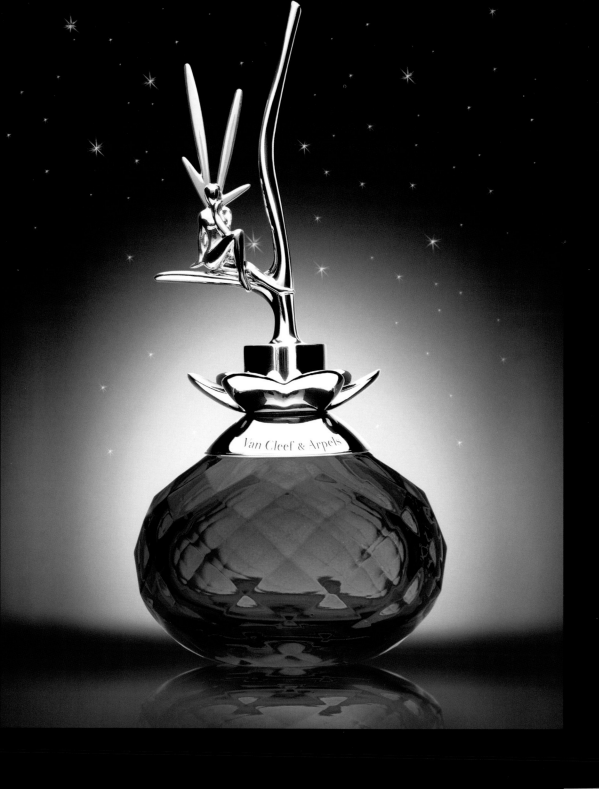

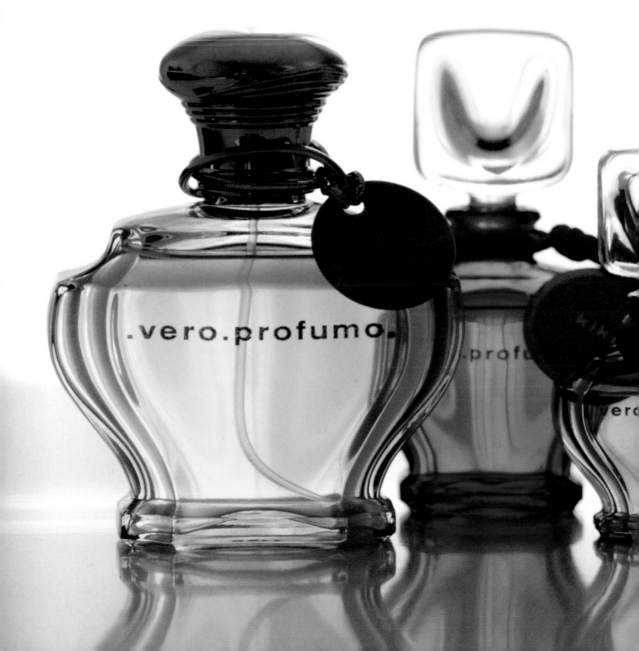

.VERO.PROFUMO.

For more than ten years now, the elegant and charismatic Vero Kern has been the strikingly creative force behind the Swiss fragrance range, vero.profumo. Having trained and worked extensively in the field of aromachology, Vero Kern is ever conscious of the important link between scent and emotional reaction. The exploration of natural raw materials was in large part responsible for her subsequent love affair with perfume and its effects on our emotions and feelings. Over time she moved naturally into perfume creation. Fascinated by the potential of combining natural and synthetic materials as a perfumer, she studied the craft in Paris for several years prior to establishing her own perfume brand – vero.profumo. This remarkable range is a happy marriage of old and new; traditional artisanal craftsmanship and contemporary high-tech processes.

Vero Kern has likened creating perfumes to "looking into a kaleidoscope, in the way that the colourful fragments constantly form and re-form amazingly beautiful and infinitely diverse pictures and patterns". There is a vivid sense of imagination and meticulous attention to detail in Vero Kern's olfactory landscapes that has resulted in a collection of exquisite, surprising and daring fragrances – Onda, Kiki and Rubj. Available as perfume extracts in 7.5ml and 15ml flacons, and eaux de parfum in 50ml spray bottles (all 100% recyclable, re-usable packaging), these three original creations promote an all encompassing concept of wellbeing. Vero Kern's deep understanding of essential oils and the unconventional combinations of high quality, pure materials lend the fragrances a uniquely aromatic signature, which some would argue can bring the wearer closer to happiness.

This sensation of happiness may in no small part be due to an underlying sensuality that comes through in the high proportion of natural oils and absolutes used in the blends. There is a real sense that each scent is intimate; tailor-made for your skin and no one else's. The first in the series, Kiki, is a dream scent for individualists who love French chic. It pays homage to the beautiful city of Paris, playing on deliciously rounded notes of caramel and musk that weave around exotic fruit leaving a devastating fragrant trail in its wake. Onda, the second scent, is an epicurean delight, oozing class and luxury through the finest vetiver and dashing touches of ginger and coriander. The most eccentric and exuberant fragrance of the range, Rubj, entices us with shimmering sweet Moroccan orange blossom, only then to seduce us with sultry jasmine and musk. The combination is effective and incredibly sensual. Vero Kern's decision to work with a blend of precious natural and synthetic materials allows her to respect the great values of established perfume traditions, as well as explore new avenues of olfactory creativity. Her distinctive character and passion for creating a deeply personal fragrance experience for all who discover her, has resulted in an outstanding collection of intimate, singular and luxurious scents for men and women. Available now worldwide and distributed through exclusive outlets, their main address CampoMarzio70 – the best known independent perfumery in Rome – has nurtured the growth of this extraordinary perfumer's living dream.

In 2004 Sergio Momo founded XerJoff International together with designer and corporate image coordinator, Dominique Salvo. They share a passion for luxury and rare perfumes which has led them to create a selection of exceptional fragrances with unique olfactory characteristics and packaging crafted from the most precious of materials. The brand's motto, 'Naturae Xquisite' (the excellence of nature) is an eloquent ode to the quest for beauty that has fuelled the work in this

astonishing collection. Mother Nature is a source of inspiration throughout each special collection – be it the scented components or the precious materials used to fashion the stunning quartz and Murano bottles. The XerJoff fragrances are created by master perfumers in the south of France and inspired by beautiful recipes and vintage formulae. The raw materials are extracted from rare plants through means of fractional distillation, making it possible to break down the scent of an ingredient into its various constituents and select only those of greatest interest according the desired result.

Sergio Momo understands that the best way to a perfume lover's heart is to fulfil the promise of beauty from the beginning to the end of his scented story. His beautiful scents are encased in jewel-like sculptured flacons. Skilled goldsmiths from Valenza Po produce the bottles from a rich variety of quartz – amethyst, lapis lazuli or Murano glass – and trim them with 18 carat gold. An African ebony base, hand carved and polished, stands as a beautiful support for each bottle.

Xerjoff's fragrances are as varied as they are beautiful but if you need to start somewhere, Shooting Stars will fire the imagination with its tales of meteorites and stardust. The collection pays homage to the wondrous meteorite shower that occurred in 1947, lighting up the sky and landing on the territory of Siberia in the Sikhote-Alin Mountains. A small Sikhote-Alin meteorite fragment – with a certificate that guarantees its origin – is inserted in a velvet envelope attached to each Shooting Star bottle. And if the individually numbered bottle doesn't make you feel special enough, the elixirs contained within certainly will. Exotic flowers, oriental spices, sun drenched citrus notes – each fragrance is as gorgeous as the next.

XERJOFF

When Xerjoff isn't lauding the merits of nature and space, it's reviving great historical formulae, notably from the respected house of Casamorati. Casamorati was established in Bologna around 1888 -La Fabbrica di Profumi C.Casamorati- and was known for its fine fragrances. XerJoff recreated two fragrances from the antique Casamorati collection, one for men – Mefisto and one for women – Fiore d'Ulivo – both rich in elegant citrus and bright floral notes from the Mediterranean.

Thanks to a deep rooted belief that the joy of scent is intrinsically linked to the wonders of nature and the beauty all around us, Xerjoff have brought a touch of magic to the world of perfume and our everyday lives.

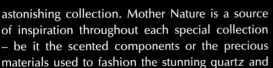

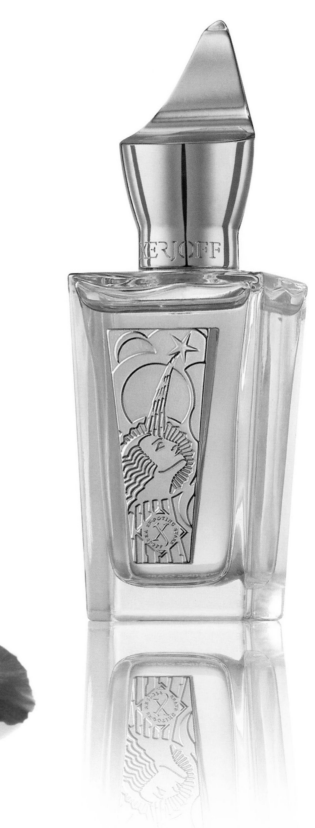
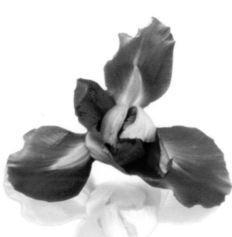

123
456
789

STRENGTH
AND APPLICATION

'WHAT TO PUT WHERE'

We have forgotten the art of perfuming ourselves. Since antiquity it was seen as an art, an obligation, a pre-requisite for refinement. But in this cash-and-carry world, driven by instant gratification and easy satiation, we find ourselves frustrated that we spend vast sums of money on smelling good but are often less than happy with our fragrant effect. Rather than getting to the root of the problem, most sales staff do not have the know-how and are ill equipped to help. So they offer suffocating blends which often asphyxiate everyone within a ten metre radius – resulting in an onset of omnosmia for the wearer combined with a palpable neurosis as people seem to flee whenever one enters a restaurant or theatre.

Having a true understanding of the strengths of scent available in the market place will allow us to achieve the fragrant effect we desire. By looking at the historical development of each product type we can see why we often find ourselves in a bit of a pickle today.

The earliest scents were made in the form of pastes or unguents. Distillation, which allowed man to remove the fragrant oils contained in certain vegetable matters had yet to be invented and so these early scents worked on the principle that fats have the ability to store odour – anyone who has placed fish alongside butter will be only too familiar with this principle. The earliest known fragrant formulae were au d'Hongrie and au de Cologne. They were relatively simple structures, where citrus and aromatic materials were steeped in alcohol resulting in a fragrant panacea which was used as a medicine, a pick-me-up and a refreshing friction for the skin. When Mr. Gillette invented the safety razor in 1900, eau de Cologne was adopted by barbers as an aftershave – the alcohol worked a mild disinfectant, and led to the product we know by that name today.

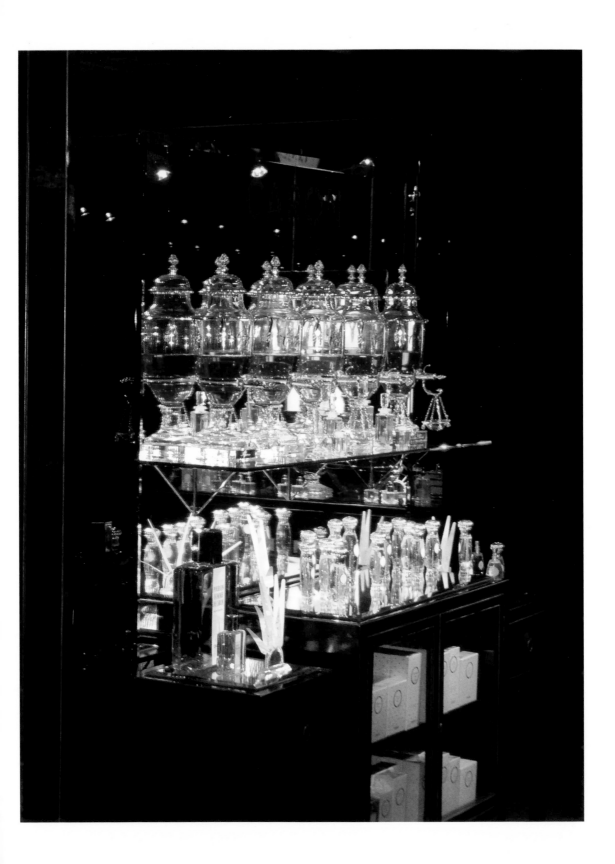

At a time when people were nervous of bathing, perfumers created a special product which is now lost to history – the scented *toile*. Although its 'fragrant echo' is left all around us. The *toile* (or fabric) underwent a long, painstaking treatment to imbibe it with scent. This process took many months and resulted in one of the ultimate luxury specialities of the fledgling perfumery industry. The dry *toile* was applied to the skin rendering it sweetly scented – or at least as sweet as it was likely to be with an absence of soap. The *toile* led to the somewhat old-fashioned word toilette, as the term used to refer to everything one did to remove the stale mal-odours of sleep. The *toile* was often used in conjunction with eau de Cologne which was applied in vast quantities as a refreshing, purifying friction. Napoleon used litres of it every day, supplied in two litre bottles known as roles. Today we have forgotten the beauty of eau de Cologne, which used to be poured into baths, poured over the body, sprinkled on bed linen and burnt in sick rooms. It is only when a smart French house launches a product by the same name and charges a fortune for it that we look at it again. But as it comes with a high price ticket, we apply it as if it were a perfume and, in doing so, totally miss the point.

The *toile* was developed by the perfumery houses and modified into an alcoholic product made to perform the same refreshing function. It became the product we know today as eau de toilette. The problem is that we have forgotten its more important relative – perfume, the name given to the product which scents or perfumes the skin. This leads to unhappy fragrant users who perceive perfume to be expensive and strong, but around 80% of an eau de toilette, will disappear within four hours; whereas a perfume will leave some 50% of its scented treasure lingering on the skin for approximately 24 hours.

To get the best effect, the eau de toilette, or its slightly more concentrated relative eau de parfum, should be applied all over the skin as a light mist. Or a more preferable way by far is to apply some in the palm of the hand before wiping it over the upper body, this will help the fragrance affix to the skin better, before applying the perfume extract. The choice of eau de toilette or eau de parfum is determined by availability. Where there is a choice, eau de parfum will give the perfume more volume; whereas eau de toilette will give a more discreet effect. Never apply scent

to the neck or to the *décolleté,* as the alcohol in it works like an astringent and can make the skin become crêpey. It is the marriage of two products, eau de toilette or eau de parfum, with perfume which makes a good fragrant effect, this in a way harks back to the alchemists who worked to create perfumes centuries ago. The aforementioned strengths will work as a background for the more refined, elegant perfume which should be applied to the wrist, the inside of the elbow and in the small dip of the collarbone directly below the earlobes. The beauty of putting scent here is that you have the pleasure of smelling it as you move your head from side-to-side, and anyone whispering sweet nothings in your ear is directly over the 'hot spot' so heaven knows where that could lead.

Hollywood taught women to apply perfume behind the ears – we produce so much sebum there – which is alkaline – that it will tend to make the scent 'turn'. Use the stopper as a dabber making sure to wipe the stopper clean. This is best done with a piece of silk, as it will remove the bodies oils and dead skin which would otherwise spoil the perfume, whilst it itself has the ability to hold scent and so when dropped inside a lingerie drawer it makes everything smell beautiful.

Sadly men generally don't have as much choice, although the principles are the same. The terms eau de toilette and eau de Cologne are blurred with companies choosing to use them in a somewhat arbitrary fashion. The real eau de Cologne was taken by men as an early aftershave, as previously mentioned, so many companies use the term because they think it sounds more masculine. It is ironic to think that the precursor to modern perfumery was Houbigant's Fougère Royale which led to Guerlain's Jicky – both were made for men and were originally made as perfume extracts. To ensure masculine sensibility is not dented, houses produce super concentrates for men, these come in many guises – extreme being the most common, with just the odd brave house creating perfumes for men. A dominant trend is for houses to make unisex or genderless compositions, the problem with these is that none come in the form of a perfume. Women, quite rightly, had their liberation, maybe this is the time for men to have theirs too.

Roja Dove

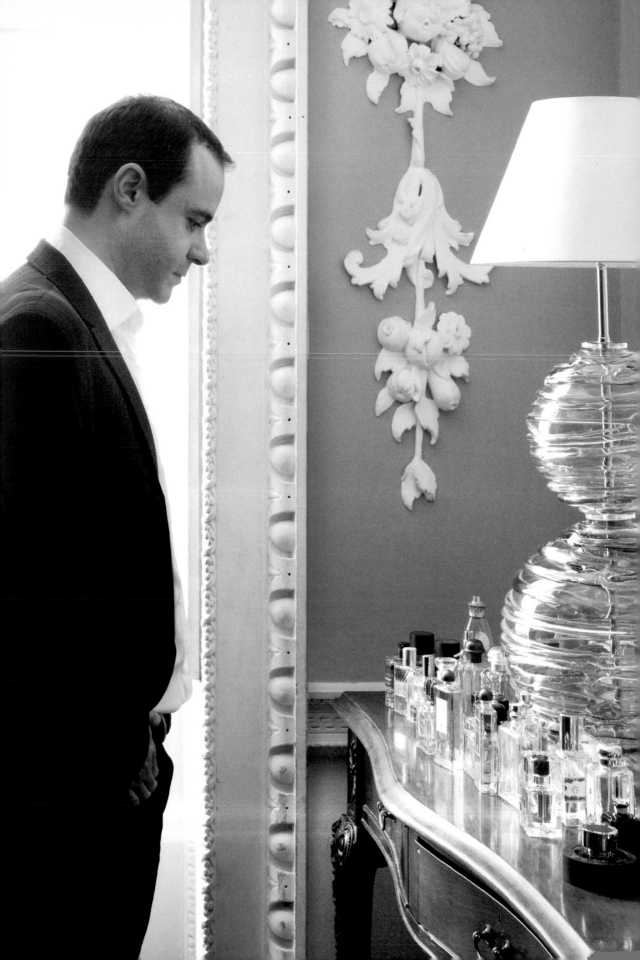

A PERFUME WARDROBE

As a perfume lover – and some would say obsessive – for many years I have had numerous love affairs with various favoured scents. Some remain memories and some are constant companions replaced immediately after the final spray is released. I have read various articles and had many discussions about finding a signature fragrance; this is certainly something I have endeavoured to do. However, I realised fairly early on and have now accepted that I am never going to be happy with only one – so my collection grows and my journey continues.

For me a perfume wardrobe is an essential addition to having a selection of clothes to choose from in the morning. Different days bring different moods and this is reflected in the way I want to scent myself for the day or evening ahead. The decision on the chosen perfume is an intuitive and emotional one, and there are certain fragrances that evoke a definite feeling and attitude in me that can match the occasion. In my collection I have firm favourites for a bright summer's day, a cold winter's night, a day of meetings in a suit and tie and one for long walks through the countryside with my dogs at my side. To me perfume is an inherent part of the way I wish to present myself to the world and how I want to feel about myself throughout the day. It is something to enjoy, to explore, to experiment with, to play with, to cherish and to enhance.

There are many opinions about the shelf life of perfume: ask around the perfume counters of a department store and speak to different people – you will hear everything from six months to eternity. In my experience, if stored out of direct sunlight and away from extremes of temperature, perfume has a very long shelf life; the principle of perfumes turning or changing is not something I have ever experienced. A shelf or two in a bedroom wardrobe is an ideal place for keeping those scented treasures; it also allows one to choose an outfit and scent at the same time. Bottles can also be kept in their boxes for added protection from the elements.

A number of years ago I was delighted to experience a fragrance journey with Roja Dove, during which I was presented with a selection of scents, each typifying a different fragrance family. Going through those presented, we discovered that I gravitated towards the chypré family. I love the enigmatic journey from this style of perfume, which starts with an initial green, fresh explosion and goes on to reveal a darker secret. In a typical chypré the top notes of citrus, herbs or florals give way to a deeper, dryer and slightly animalic heart and base, slowly unfolding with complexities and layers of mystery and sensuality.

Photo by Paul Raeside

During a typical work day with meetings and appointments, being dressed in a suit and tie, a fresh and clean fragrance is the perfect match. Eau d' Hermès does the job and also represents my love of chyprés perfectly. What starts off as a blast of fresh citrus soon develops into a darker herbal and leather journey that lasts throughout the day. Eau d'Hermès is the first fragrance from Hermès, created by Edmond Roudnitska in 1951. Roudnitska was one of the greatest perfumers ever to have lived and this creation still feels modern and relevant, all the while exuding old school class.

For a spring or summer's day Jo Malone's Amber & Lavender is a superb, clean, powerful scent that adds a beautiful blast of fresh air to cut through the city's heat. This scent hides a trick or two as it unfolds: what starts off as a smart, fresh, somewhat simple scent develops into a closer, enveloping skin scent with nods to the orient. Jo Malone's fragrances have a sophisticated excellence, often built around cleverly paired accords, to create perfumes that have a luminance, clarity and an aura of quality.

A colder day may see me reaching for Ormonde Man, by London-based Ormonde Jayne. Ormonde Man begins with similar freshness and formalness but adds depth of warmth and comfort to the mix; another chypré, this one ventures into uncharted territory using a note of hemlock along with the Arabian note of precious oud. These rare and unusual ingredients add to the magic and allure and have me regularly sniffing at my wrist when wearing it.

Special occasions call for special fragrances – an invitation to a smart restaurant or event and I typically go for the 'big guns' in my wardrobe. The Clive Christian for Men trilogy is my favoured heavy artillery. The three scents have a wonderfully persuasive presence and a quality and tenacity that slowly unravels throughout the day, giving the most incredible aura of luxury. X for Men is seriously sexy whilst retaining true elegance. X contains high concentrations of the finest ingredients but, rather than overpower by shouting about its rare and expensive components, it is confident enough to stay close to the skin and quietly advertise that this is a V8 Turbo of a male fragrance.

Evenings may begin with a friend over a drink at a hotel bar and then on to dinner; for this a darker and stronger scent seems appropriate. During the winter months a good choice would be the rubber intensity of Bulgari Black. This unisex oriental mixes almost industrial rubber accords with smoky deep Lapsang tea notes to amazing effect. Dzing by l'Artisan Parfumeur has a similar strength and appeal but this time leather is the note played out. This Olivia Giacobetti creation has the circus as its muse; the leather accord in Dzing definitely has a hint of animal within its journey. Both of these unusual and heady scents add an irresistible layer of warmth and an interesting depth to an evening out. For a warmer summer's night out I lean towards a more playful scent that contains some fruit and floral accords: Dior Homme with the lush deep iris along with rich fruit is a great choice.

There is a collection that I never stay away from for long, the Escentric Molecules quartet is a firm favourite. Wear them during the day or night, for the office or for play, either in or out, they just work. Molecule 01 is the leader of the pack with the mysterious ebbs and flows that the unique high concentrations of Iso E Super resonate. This molecule used in its singularity has an effect that is almost magical. Layering the collection adds to its seductive and alluring nature: my favoured combination is Molecule 01 with Escentric 02.

Weekends and holidays open up yet more options: there are scents that vividly bring back a time and a place. Duty free purchases prior to flying off on holiday have fixed certain smells deep in my mind and forever linked them to a faraway city or resort. Jo Malone's Pomegranate Noir will always remind me of a balmy Hong Kong August – a few sprays take me straight there. Hermès' Jardin collection brings back days relaxing and exploring the Mediterranean; it has such a leisurely and indulgent quality that perfectly encapsulate the feeling of being on holiday for me. Eau du Sud by Annick Goutal will take me to small towns in Provence in an instant – such a sunny scent with a beautiful citrus and herbal blend. During a weekend away from home in colder weather I will need a warmer, comforting scent with a deep and enveloping quality. Ideal for taking a crisp walk through the autumn leaves would be one of the classics from Guerlain or Robert Piguet – give me Jicky or Bandit for times like these.

There are definite styles and characteristics that draw me to fragrances and my collection illustrates this: chyprés feature most heavily, from the leathery and animalic to the green freshness of herbals and citruses. One ingredient always gets my attention – vetiver, distilled from the roots of a tall grass that originated in India, though now the best is sourced from Réunion and Haiti. The complexities and dualities of this ingredient draw me in, at once clean and soapy whilst being smoky and earthy. It is the perfect masculine accord and can work just as well with a suit in the boardroom as with jeans and t-shirt at the weekend. Lubin has a wonderful vetiver comparable to the finest Cognac served in a heavy crystal glass. Miller Harris's Vetiver Bourbon is a woodier, darker and earthier working that is powerful and will certainly last all day. Vetiver from Guerlain is probably the best known; a classic since its launch in 1959, the clean, soapy almost edible side of this ingredient is at work here.

As I continue to wear and enjoy fragrance, my journey of discovery develops: however loyal I am to my firm favourites, I love to try new offerings regularly and remain excited at new releases. My wardrobe will, no doubt, continue to grow and I will find new companions for the different and special times in my life. Fragrances give my life a special dimension of pleasure and that layer of luxury and beauty is something I love and cherish. I would encourage anyone who is married to their one and only favourite perfume to go and explore and enjoy the world of scent that is out there, and find their own collection of fragrant lovers to accompany them.

Anton Mossa

123
456
789

THE CREATIVES

CAMILLE GOUTAL AND ISABELLE DOYEN

Camille became Artistic Creative Director for the Annick Goutal perfume house after her mother Annick passed away at the end of the 1990s. Isabelle Doyen graduated from the ISIPCA perfumery school of Paris in 1982 and then went on to work as an assistant to Annick Goutal, continuing this work as a perfumer with Camille thereafter. Together they have collaborated on some successful and beautiful fragrances for the range. Apart from over 20 creations for Annick Goutal, Isabelle has worked for other fragrance houses, namely Les Nez, and trained some of today's most admired noses through her association with ISIPCA. Camille's earlier passion for photography is equaled by her passion for fragrance to stunning effect.

I started by asking them about their most recent collaboration – Ninfeo mio – inspired by the spectacular Giardino di Ninfa; a garden near Rome which is occasionally open to the public.

Camille – Isabelle and I had both dreamed of exploring verbena as a raw material but with the advent of industry regulations restricting its use in fragrances we were forced to rethink our approach. We had ideas brewing for something involving a citrus based garden, The Garden of the Hesperides. It was by chance that we learned of this wonderful garden near Rome. It was beautifully preserved and yet wild and lush at the same time. It became clear that we could incorporate another vision into our initial dream. We set about exploring the fragrant qualities of the fig and crisp green notes; of aquatic and milky touches, so mouth watering and fresh. We realised there were ways to combine fresh citrus notes into all this and to achieve a similar effect to what we had originally sought. So it evolved reflecting the beauty of the river coursing through that garden.

Q   How does your partnership work?

Camille – We have known each other for years as Isabelle worked with my mother Annick and so I have always had Isabelle around me. It was a natural progression for us to take on my mother's legacy. Isabelle has given me confidence; she has taught me a lot and been extremely supportive and encouraging. I had always been surrounded by perfume, I was wearing La Nuit by Paco Rabanne by the time I was ten – quite an adult scent to say the least – so in a sense I wasn't even aware of the osmosis taking place as a I got older, it was just there. Although my interest and work had been with photography before working with Isabelle, it felt natural.

Isabelle — We have very similar ideas about fragrances. We rarely disagree, quite the opposite, though our tastes can be different, we spark off each other. You should see us working together! Sometimes when we've been given a brief for our next fragrance and even though we know we have deadlines to meet, we'll still be busy exploring and changing, experimenting and perfecting with only a month to go. It gets to the point where people are pulling their hair out around us telling us to get a move on! I guess you could say we are never short of inspiration together!

Q How do you feel once your perfume is finished and released into the world?

Camille — Once it's out there, it's done. I am quite used to that part of things now so I am no longer as nervous as you would imagine.

Isabelle — I tend to feel relieved because it's invariably been quite a journey, a lot of work to get there. Sometimes later on down the line, maybe five years later, I smell one of our creations and think, " That's pretty good even if I do say so myself! How am I going to top that?"

Q What are your favourite Annick Goutal scents, or the ones that mark you, and where do you draw inspiration from?

Camille – I love white flowers in particular. My favourite scent from Annick Goutal is Songes. It means a lot to me as it was the first scent I created, with its white flowers and powdery touch. It reminds me of my honeymoon in Mauritius where the night air was laced with the heady scent of frangipani flowers all around. My mother was very fond of roses and Ce Soir ou Jamais was a real tribute to that flower. She worked strenuously on this composition even whilst ill (it was her last creation before she died), determined to capture her perfect rose, one that she had smelled years before in the south of France. It's a striking scent that reminds me of my mother so much. Another link between mother and love – when I was barely out of my teens I was lucky enough to have my mother create Petite Chérie for me. It means 'Little Darling' in French and is a symbol of a mother's love for her child. You could say that love is a constant theme throughout our fragrances.

My travels can inspire me, although I would never say that I have to go to the end of the earth to seek inspiration or to find the perfect raw material. Yes, these things can help, but really there is such a wealth of materials available to us now that our imagination and lives are the real key to interesting ideas. I could find inspiration at home, in Paris or in London, which is one of my favourite cities. I used to live there and I love its energy, colour, the feeling that anybody or anything goes. There is room for creativity and that is very freeing.

Isabelle – I live and smell things all the time; it is all consuming you could say. But nature really influences me, as well as the places and people I love. Even smells that could make me feel sad, melancholy or nostalgic have their place; it could be the smell of pencil shavings, violets, iris or even of the swimming pool. Every smell has something interesting to offer.

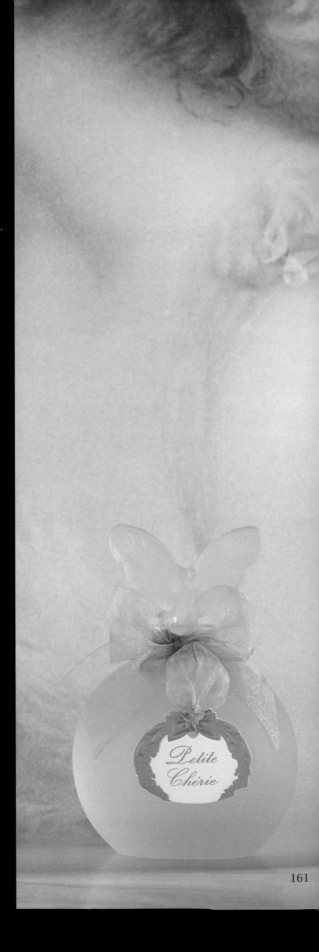

How important is contact with your audience? You have made appearances in perfume stores and boutiques at various times to present a fragrance or talk to customers.

Camille – Yes it is important and very interesting to meet people who wear your fragrances or who are seeking their signature scent. It's my chance to guide them through the collection and listen to them. To help them discover less usual scents and highlight the importance of taking your time when choosing your fragrance as it will invariably unfold over several hours. This especially is important for some of the more complex fragrances which may get neglected because they aren't instantly obvious and may not get the exposure they deserve. For example Eau de Camille or Heure Exquise are in turn, striking and natural, velvety and enveloping but these qualities, which make them so wearable, need time to breathe on the skin. It's frustrating at times and can lead to scents being discontinued unfortunately, but that's the way it goes.* (see below for reference).

What does the future hold for Annick Goutal fragrances?

Camille – We will continue to create and be inspired by our experiences and we are lucky to have the audience and the demand for these. There are plans to branch out and build on the romantic world we stand for and pay homage to feminine beauty with some surprises in store. It promises to be exciting and lovely!

Isabelle – I shall continue to work with passion as I always have. I derive pleasure from seeing students of mine now successfully carving their own niche in the world of perfume. There is still a lot to do; perfume is a never ending journey.

*(At this point we spoke about an Annick Goutal scent that no longer exists. I had worn it religiously in the past and I missed it a lot; Des Lys, a beautiful lily scent. Every time I wore it, strangers would literally stop me in the street to compliment me or ask me what it was. I finished our interview only to find that Isabelle had disappeared to make a little bottle of it up for me from memory. The joys of perfume are never ending.)

JEAN-FRANÇOIS LATTY

Jean-François Latty started his career in 1965 when he entered a very famous perfumery school in Grasse. His creations include Givenchy III, YSL for Men (Yves Saint Laurent) and he founded his own company in 2000, specialising in perfume creation and selling natural ingredients. After several years' absence he stepped back into the world of perfume when he met Caroline Ilacqua and was introduced to the Téo Cabanel collection.

Jean-François Latty: I first met Caroline in 2002 when she was visiting Grasse with her mother, at that time the collection was still a work in progress. I considered reworking the existing formulae but upon reflection, I decided it would be preferable to start afresh with new fragrances rather than revisit old ones.

The fragrances are elegant, refined and rich. They pay homage to the school of *haute parfumerie* in the same vein as Chanel, Guerlain and Dior. The current collection is sufficiently varied as to appeal to a wide cross-section of women without compromising that distinctive Téo Cabanel signature. The first two fragrances came from my own ideas; however the following two fragrances saw me joining forces with Caroline. My working methods can vary and the first two fragrances came from a precise idea I already had in my head. I can, however, sometimes draw inspiration from outside influences – other scents, things I have seen or Mother Nature even.

It's incredibly gratifying to smell your fragrance on people around you, but in reality the success of a perfume relies on so many other factors too, including the packaging, the image... Some of my fragrances haven't achieved the success expected of them, either because the brand wasn't sufficiently well known, or because the fragrance itself was maybe a little ahead of its time. However, inversely, when I have sent someone an anonymous bottle of one of my fragrances, the wearer has loved it and asked for another bottle, which serves to underline the influence that marketing has on the success and lifespan of a fragrance.

The perfume industry today has been taken over by a cluster of large companies whose massive marketing campaigns command huge financial investment. Subsequently the perfume creator's freedom is greatly reduced due to heavy costs incurred elsewhere. Add to this recent restraints imposed by governing bodies such as IFRA, resulting in thousands of materials being removed from use or greatly limited, and yet again creativity is the first thing to be sacrificed.

When I was training to become a perfumer, I studied eight hours a day for a year before being tutored by a number of great perfume masters. It took me ten years to truly qualify as a professional perfumer. Nowadays, young creators take a few classes a week covering a number of topics including marketing and toxicology research, before being thrust into the work place. They then have to compete with dozens or hundreds of other perfumers in order to sell their fragrance idea to a firm in record time, in order to meet the demands of a rapid turnover market. There is simply no time to create and research when making a perfume in this manner.

Whereas in the past, we would see maybe 50 new fragrances emerge on the market every year, now we see 500! Where a fragrance would expect to live at least 15 to 20 years, now we're lucky if a fragrance lives longer than two years. Customers become disillusioned and disappointed, and they stop buying - it's easy to see why. We've reached a stage where every day products, like Camay and Lux soap, have more continuity to them!

This is why the possibility of working with Téo Cabanel was such a gift. I equate my need for creativity with that of an artist able to paint what inspires them in their own time and in the privacy of their workshop. Freedom is the key to good perfume, not profitability or financial gain.

CHRISTINE NAGEL CREATES A NEW INTENSITY FOR JO MALONE

"A fashion show. A painting. An opera. Even a flower in the middle of concrete. Anything in life can be a source of inspiration to me," explains Christine Nagel, the multi-award winning perfumer with whom the Jo Malone Creative Studio has chosen to collaborate on some of its most recent and compelling innovations. "But most of the time, it is meeting people that inspire me," she adds. "I create fragrances for people."

Nagel also creates perfumes of distinction, drawn as she is to ingredients of unparalleled quality. And she admits to being positively audacious in her choice - and use - of those ingredients. "I am a risktaker. Daring. Not safe. But for me, innovation springs from the blending of authentic ingredients. I like to surprise with simple things."

Such sensibility is spot on for Jo Malone. The British luxury perfume house is renowned for its beautifully crafted fragrances characterised by simplicity and transparency as well as a certain fearlessness; an unexpected touch that delivers a little gasp-factor and draws you in. Then keeps you addicted.

It is also famous for its ethos of fragrance combining. Each Jo Malone Cologne has been structured so it can be worn solo as a sublime statement of singular elegance or layered for endless bespoke effects. "This is innovative. There are no limits," says Nagel, "it's a creative thread that runs through the brand."

Dominic De Vetta, Global General Manager, heads up the Jo Malone Creative Studio; "We work with a stable of prestigious perfumers and there was a precision about Christine's work that resonated with us and suggested she was absolutely right to help us create Cologne Intense. This is our new collection inspired by venerable ingredients used in Middle Eastern perfumery but shot through with a fresh luminosity that makes them unequivocally modern and unmistakably Jo Malone."

In Nagel's hands, time-honoured ingredients have been tantalisingly transformed, and tradition seamlessly segues with the zeitgeist. The quartet – Amber & Patchouli, Oud & Bergamot, Rose Water & Vanilla and Iris & White Musk – are rich, deep and intoxicatingly resonant, yet illuminated by a crisp contemporary clarity.

"Each ingredient has a reason for being," says Nagel. "Nothing is superfluous. Yes, it's a bold approach, but I wanted to take such risks to create fragrances with impact and heart. I chose to take potentially opposing ingredients of very high quality to create unexpected yet harmonious fragrances."

The result is an oud, still smoky and mysterious but with a dazzling translucence. Sweet vanilla and rose water have been spiked with neroli to give a certain edge and, likewise, creamy white musk is partnered with an airy, powdery iris root so it dances with a new diaphanous dimension.

"With amber and patchouli, you have two very different and strong ingredients that could clash," she continues. "But I have blended them harmoniously so that the amber melts into the patchouli, which I've given a more supple, suede like quality thanks to molecular distillation."

Nagel knows more about molecules than most, having started out in the field of 'chromatography' – a scientific discipline that separates out the minute constituents of a mixture for analysis. "I had to smell 'finished' fragrances and pinpoint the formula. It wasn't a creative job – in fact, it was very technical – but it has given me the desire to look for new accords, new associations and create sense-pleasing unions. It was an experience that has undoubtedly assisted me with my perfumery."

What has also helped is her family heritage, being half Swiss and half Italian: "I have two facets influencing my personality and my way of working – the perfect balance of rigour and discipline combined with spontaneity and audacity," she says.

Indeed, Nagel believes that brave, beautifully crafted fragrances that have the power to touch people's lives emerge from creative freedom. That fragrances with soul are dreamt up in the imagination, not thrashed out in the board room. And that Jo Malone allows her the scope to experiment and share in an inspiring two-way process with the Jo Malone Creative Studio.

"I am always instinctive and I am very intuitive. Perfumery is not intellectual. It is emotional. It is something really deep and intimate," Nagel concludes. "When fragrance elicits an emotion, the adventure begins." And with the introduction of soul-stirring, pulse-quickening Cologne Intense, the Jo Malone story continues to unfold.

Interview by Jan Masters

◎ Is your personal reaction to each scent crucial to the design of the bottles or do you aim for a more abstract product?

My bottle designs are not that specific but generally there is a commonality to the design – a house feel, as with the perfumes in my collection there is a house accord of rose and jasmine at the heart of each scent, there is also continuity with the bottle design. 1872, a perfume named as a tribute to the year Queen Victoria granted her crown to each bottle in the perfumery, is housed in a green bottle authentic to the original style of the house. When I designed a crystal bottle for the Pure Perfumes in the collection I designed what I saw as the most reverent vessel for a perfume of this quality.

CLIVE CHRISTIAN

◎ What is your greatest source of inspiration?

History. The perfumes in the Clive Christian collection take inspiration from the archives of The Crown Perfumery and are brought up to date. The bottles that house the perfumes follow the same philosophy – they are taken from history and given an elegant modern twist. The Perfume Spray bottles are created using the original press and you can still see the seam where the glass is pressed together – it is authentic.

◎ Your designs and style exude sophistication and luxury but how important are these qualities in your own enjoyment of fragrance in general. Does one have go with the other for the overall effect to be complete?

Absolutely yes – what you see and feel must be in tandem with the smell – if it doesn't connect then it wouldn't be right. It would be a disappointment. A good example in my own work is the application of a diamond onto the collar of the No.1 Pure Perfume as an indicator that what is inside the bottle is out of the ordinary – the most precious natural gem and the most precious natural ingredients.

◎ Could you explain to our readers which particular experiences or moment sealed your decision to revive and develop the Crown Perfumery fragrances formula?

As the founder of Clive Christian Furniture we have built a bespoke design company that manufactures in the United Kingdom and supplies the most luxurious homes around the world. In the 1970s we transformed the perception of the kitchen from a functional workspace to a room that is celebrated and enjoyed. The moment that sealed the decision for me to move into the discipline of perfume was when I looked at The Crown Perfumery, what they were, where they had come from and what they had allowed themselves to become – and then I looked at the market and realised that fragrance was severely undervalued. It had become a mass-marketed, gimmicky thing and it needed to re-establish its roots as one of the most luxurious items that can be indulged in. We did this immediately, releasing our definitive collection in 1999, and haven't moved an inch or been deflected from our vision since we launched ten years ago. Although Clive Christian Perfume was initially berated, the industry has now significantly moved on.

How does luxury and design in Britain fare today? Vintage or historical British fragrance bottles have struggled at times to keep up with the times so how can you maintain that sense of heritage whilst remaining vital and relevant?

At Clive Christian we don't 'do' fashion. 'Vintage' is now being presented as a fashionable item and therefore it will be at the mercy of the current trends. We have never presented ourselves as being fashionable hence we are timeless and hence we stand the test of time.

What are your proudest achievements and what would you like to be able to throw yourself into in the future? Do you have any dream collaborations or fragrances you can share with us?

In retrospect I am very pleased that the Clive Christian revival of the spirit of luxury perfume has been so well received across the World and the customer is now more educated in their choice of perfume and so the industry at large has responded. I was very proud to be commissioned to design a unique bottle for HM Queen Elizabeth II on the occasion of her Golden Jubilee which was unveiled at the V&A museum – I chose the shape of a crown, in deference to the crown that Queen Victoria had given to the perfumery in 1872, and filled it with No.1 The Worlds Most Expensive Perfume. I feel I have already achieved my dream collaboration by working with Baccarat on the limited edition bottle of No.1 Perfume – the 'Imperial Majesty' – which was given a unique award by the Fragrance Foundation for Outstanding Perfume Presentation.

Clive, I'd like to finish by asking what you think is the secret to the success of such a luxurious collection in today's modern economic world? Is it all about escapism?

Things that purport to being luxury do well when the economy is booming – everyone does well then. True luxury maintains its position regardless of the economy as people are more selective and more considered – this is when true luxury shines through and this is what 'Clive Christian' stands for. Design it to be the very best that it can be – then cost it. Design first, always.

THE ART & SOUND OF PERFUME

A student performs a perfume composition

The Sound Of Perfume Judges join winning composer Ikoyu Kobayashi

As creators of a definitive collection of British luxury perfume Clive Christian understand that perfume can be appreciated on many levels and that the true way to experience the complexities of pure perfume is by investing in the most concentrated form of the scent – in a crystal stopper bottle.

When a drop of perfume is placed on the skin in this fashion the perfume is allowed to slowly begin its journey. The perfume unravels on the skin revealing all the facets and intricacies as it warms; capturing memories and moments within each note that can last a lifetime. It is much like hearing a piece of music for the first time that strikes a chord in your soul and becomes a cherished anthem in the soundtrack of your life.

Clive Christian Perfume brought both these disciplines together in an award-winning project called 'The Sound of Perfume'. Students at The Royal College of Music were challenged to bring the perfumes to life with the notes of music. The students were blindfolded to enhance their focus on their sense of smell and then Clive Christian No1 – advertised as The World's Most Expensive Perfume was fanned around the room. The students were then asked to consider their first impressions of the perfume and translate their experience of the olfactory notes – the whirl of emotions that their heads and hearts had been filled with and the scents that their noses had been immersed in – into a musical composition.

Nine finalist compositions were played to 500 guests at the Britten Theatre, London. The audience, including patrons of the Royal College and guests of Clive Christian Perfume, were taken on a sensory journey; as they were plunged into darkness the perfume was wafted through the auditorium and each composition was performed.

The winning piece in 'The Sound of Perfume', chosen by judges Lord Robert Winston, composer Debbie Wiseman, editor Gillian de Bono and creator of No1 Clive Christian was 'Stay Gold', composed by Ikoyu Kobayashi. This piece has since been performed at Cadogan Hall, London and at the most exclusive private members club in Palm Beach, Mar A Lago, filling the air with music and perfume. To listen to the winning piece of music created in honour of Clive Christian No1 visit www.thesoundofperfume.com

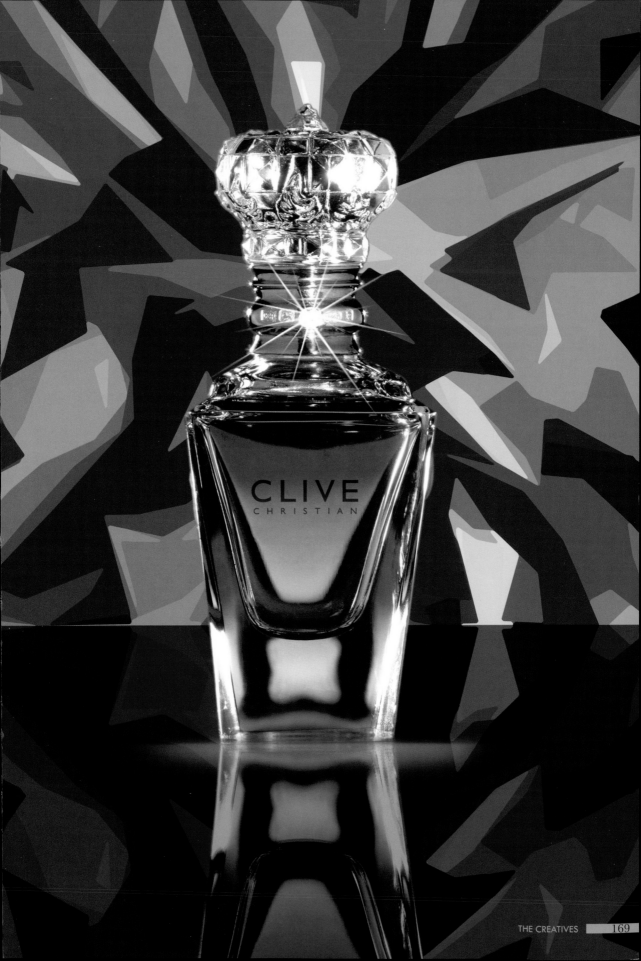

Q Paul, you are involved in the design of packaging for the fragrance brand Escentric Molecules. Can you explain how the creation process came about?

It all started with a conversation between Geza (the nose behind Escentric Molecules), Jeff Lounds (branding expert from This Company) and myself. A brief tour around the concept of an homage to a single aroma chemical, followed by the working versions of Molecule 01 and Escentric 01.

For Me Company it rapidly developed as investigations into concepts that could be loosely described as binary efflorescence, the science of a scent, and the sensuality of encoded messaging.

We had 0 & 1 on our minds – everything decodable if looked at intelligently enough. An arcane, submerged string of messages about the product. The 01s are more dense than the 02s, but even the dots on the 02s are decipherable. All of this was a distinct and clear response to the nature of fragrance and its role in attraction.

We have a saying – "Being creative is like running in someone else's trainers. You don't know where you're going all the time. You don't think about thinking, the synapses fire and you feel possessed. It's like speaking in tongues".

Q Working with such an intangible and deeply personal product as fragrance, does this add to the challenge set before you or do you find it liberating?

Not when it's this fragrance. It was very liberating from the outset. As we progress further with new Escentric Molecules concepts it still is.

PAUL WHITE
ME COMPANY

◻ Where do you draw your influences from in your work? Obviously with Escentric Molecule's, you must have had reaction to the scent, was this crucial to you in this instance?

It was more a reaction to the concept of the scent that drove the creative process than the scent 'speaking' to us as such.

Mainly our influences come from experimentation. This is clearly visible in our work, it's something that we do because we are optimistic about the future. What we try to produce are designs that synthesise this enthusiasm for modernity, to produce something fresh and vital for our clients.

The ability to experiment is something more valuable than money in many, many ways and this is why Me Company has never limited itself to just doing one thing. Over the history of the company we have spent more than 15 years designing packaging for recording artists; set up a character design studio; conceptualised and directed music promos; created an abstract animated film that we projected up onto the roof of a disused planetarium in Tokyo; published a book about our work; held exhibitions around the world, conceptualised and shot fashion campaigns; designed the first designer bar in London, to name but a few!

It's important to note that we often don't develop ideas with a specific outlet for that work in mind, the process is on-going and organic. There are ideas on the website that have no client basis, nor are they conceived solely as images, they are conceived and exist for the idea alone. Me Company's work is influenced by a hedonistic desire to go as far as you can with an idea and then to look hard for ways of pushing it even more.

As in the case of Escentric Molecules, where someone really wants to work with you simply because they like and trust your potential to produce something original, this is going to produce the most interesting and original work.

◻ What are your proudest achievements and what would you like to be able to throw yourself into in the future? Do you have any dream collaborations you can share with us?

Me Company is 25 years old. A lot of the Me Company archive is really special to me, far too much to pick something out, so I guess I would have to say that the archive is my proudest achievement. Our Exhibition at G2 in Tokyo with our animated film presentation at a disused planetarium in Tokyo, and the publication of our book Luminous all at the same time. Plus our exhibition at Visionaire in New York, all must also rate very highly for me. The success of Escentric Molecules and the launch of Beautiful Mind I would also consider great achievements.

◻ And finally Paul what do you think is the secret to the success of such a collection and brand as Escentric Molecules and its brand image?

Possibly the dark, encoded packaging has a quiet dignity that speaks to people. Equally the restraint of the branding and the subtle encoding help with the idea of a personal possession of the brand - we have heard people say many times that it is their fragrance and not ours.

BERTRAND DUCHAUFOUR

Bertrand Duchaufour is a French perfume creator whose fragrances have breathed life and excitement into an astounding and eclectic array of brand portfolios over the decades. For perfume aficionados he will need no introduction, but suffice to say, he is the great nose and mind behind such wonders as: Jubilation XXV for Amouage; Amaranthine for Penhaligon's; Dzongkha for l'Artisan Parfumeur; and Avignon for Comme des Garçons, to name but a few.

Q   Bertrand Duchaufour, you have created fragrances for some of the world's most respected perfume houses; each very distinct in their style and image. How much of yourself do you bring to your creations or are you able to detach yourself totally for the purpose of professional impartiality?

No, I don't think any so called artist can create without contributing a part of themselves to the work. More and more perfume houses deploy a particular method of creation which only serves to underline why my own work should be respected... I stay true to my spirit, my way of thinking and my convictions. Respect is crucial with my clients too. The perfectly impartial and clinical work carried out in the factories for the big brands is so far removed from me and what I am. That's far behind me, in the past.

Q   Your creations can be dark and sensual, delicate and airy; natural and clear or abstract and mysterious. Would you say you are all these things too in your everyday life?

Yes I am definitely a mass of contrasting character traits. I'm not easy to approach, definitely not easy to live or work with, but that's how it is! *A prendre ou à laisser* as the French say! (Take me or leave me!)

Q   Obviously scent is related to human reaction and I wonder which emotions, situations and places you find the most inspirational?

All emotions inspire me. One thing that's certain is that situations and places engender emotions. The more these circumstances move me, the more inspired I become and feel.

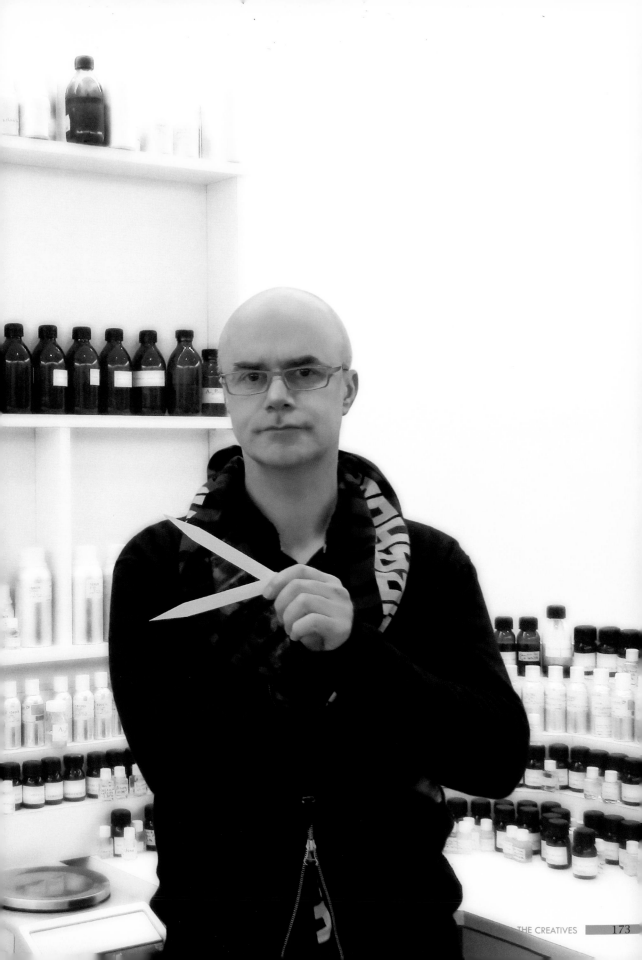

Q How does it feel to witness the effect your fragrances have on other people?

Clearly satisfying! I remember someone (a man!) crying after smelling one of my creations that had actually been inspired by one of his own works of art- a sculpture. That was only one person's reaction but it was such a huge display of gratitude.

Q Which moment in your life defined your destiny as a perfumer?

When I arrived in Grasse to begin my professional life. That was the very precise moment, on the first day I arrived in that town.

Q Is there a perfume that can literally stop you in your tracks and bring tears to your eyes or give you goose pimples just from one sniff? Can you tell us your all time most precious scents or fragrances?

Some fragrances have impressed me a lot, but it's mostly for nostalgic reasons. For example Mitsouko, Femme de Rochas and Dior Homme really impress me because of their huge nostalgic power. Anything that relates back to the ancient period of perfume history; the very beginning of modern perfumery (the first half of the 20th century). I always associate this historic period of perfumery with certain old movies, with beautiful actresses – Greta Garbo, Marlene Dietrich, Gene Tierney – as I do also with certain fashion creators like Dior and Balenciaga at their dizzy heights. They symbolise a certain elegance, a particularly French elegance, and they relate to my deep rooted childhood memories... to an unconscious memory, I am sure... A part of me that I don't want to unveil, for fear of erasing the magic of my life-long, everlasting dream...

Q Would you say you are always completely satisfied with every one of your creations and of which are you the proudest?

No, I am definitely not. One thing that's certain though – the more personal my involvement in what I've done, the more coherent and the closer the result is to what I set out to achieve.

Q What it is about perfume that speaks to you and makes you want to create?

The process of interest is very unusual and unconscious as I said. I try not to let existing fragrances inspire me. I try to find new means of discovery. The raw materials I use day after day in my lab are a fantastic source of inspiration. I can discover new facets to the products I use (mainly natural ones) on a daily basis and the obvious chemistry/synergy they produce can very often hit my olfactory senses like an explosion. Also, Mother Nature herself. Da Vinci said that nature is the eternal and limitless fountain of revelations, harmony and inspiration. Why not make use of these? He was so right. A journey, simply a path across some country fields, can yield so many ideas in just a matter of minutes!

Q Finally Bertrand, can you give us an insight into what the future holds for us as your fans? Do you have projects you still dream of fulfilling in the pipeline?

Sure! A lot of projects for a lot of brands. My main work- with Penhaligon's- is centred around the atmosphere of a tailor's workshop and broaches the relatively new concept of a traditional fougère with very special note blends. For l'Artisan Parfumeur; I am working on the theme of the tuberose flower (a very special tuberose) and the city of Istanbul. But I am also working for some very small brands that have given me amazingly free reign- a very challenging process which I find as intensely pleasing as what I am doing in my more high profile partnerships.

LINDA PILKINGTON

Founder of Ormonde Jayne

◎ Linda, How difficult is it to stick to your principles as an artisanal perfumer nowadays and could you explain what the pitfalls and advantages are?

The single most important aspect for Ormonde Jayne is never to compromise our core principles and philosophy, even if this means lower margins or slower growth. This is what sets us apart and what we are known for. We feel that this, more than ever, is the time for such unrelenting focus on quality and personal service. The high end of the luxury market is, today, leaning ever more towards true quality and craftsmanship whether it be a boutique perfumery, Saville Row suits, hand made shoes or delightful artisanal chocolatiers...

Ormonde Jayne seeks to use rare and unusual oils that are not widely used in the perfume industry today. The advantage is that most perfume houses don't want to spend that kind of budget on the ingredients. They are typically large corporates or private equity backed businesses looking constantly to maximise financial returns. We realise that we are a small player without the marketing power, and therefore we need to differentiate ourselves in other ways – by investing in our products and packaging to grow our customer following and brand for the long-term. The pitfall, other than the higher cost of production, is that we may discover a fabulous new flower but then encounter logistical difficulties in sourcing and production, for example, if the farmer is located half way up a mountain in Colombia. In certain cases, we have waited eight months for flowers to be picked and the oil extracted, which is clearly not ideal.

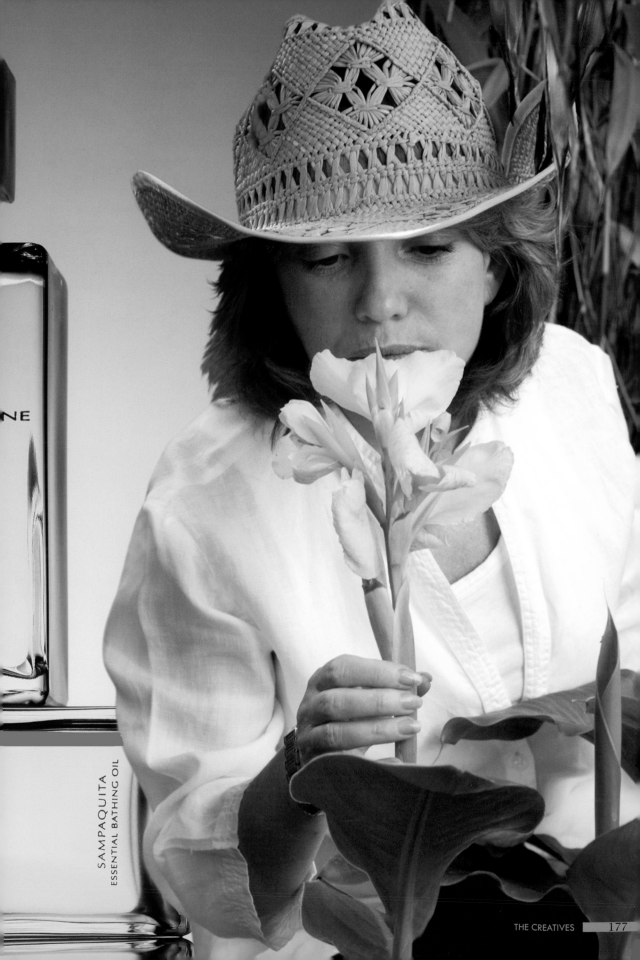

SAMPAQUITA
ESSENTIAL BATHING OIL

Q Could you run through a day or two in your life for us and give us a little insight into your daily work?

To own and run a perfume house sounds so romantic but as we manufacture our own products, our studio is like a miniature laboratory, factory and distribution centre, all rolled into one. I go there twice a week to check our orders and make sure we have all the stock needed. Creating from scratch requires a very organised stock take. The candles and bathing oils are made by Sashalee – who has worked alongside me since I moved Ormonde Jayne from my home almost ten years ago – while I am fully personally responsible for the perfumes. The back room is cooled and darkened, which is optimal for fine fragrance, and we keep the perfumes in 5 kilo vats. I check them to make sure the liquid is clear and compound any perfume that is running low.

Our Bond Street store is a 20 minute drive away from both the studio and from my home in Primrose Hill. My main focus here is product development, so my office is full of oils, materials, soap formulations, new bottles, tubes and anything I have requested samples of. There is a big mood board where I pin all my new ideas when feeling inspired. I am very keen to innovate, so here I constantly think about and plan new ideas for the following year or two.

Q Which aspect of your work do you derive the most pleasure from?

The most exciting part is to either have some lovely new oil samples to play with or to have hit upon a new idea that I am putting together – where it has not been done in the industry yet, I can hardly contain myself. While it is great to receive critical acclaim or be featured in a nice magazine, I derive even greater personal satisfaction in meeting people who enjoy our products, whether buying them or receiving them as gifts - their praise and love for our products is probably the single most rewarding aspect of what I do.

Q As your company expands through popular demand how do you see developments moving whilst respecting your philosophy? Is it possible to marry commercial success with personal control and decision making?

I am very clear on how far I can take Ormonde Jayne and I know what our capacity is before we have to relook at

how we do things. As far as I am concerned, I will be in control for many years to come because we do not have external investors and almost no debt, so therefore, no expansion obligation or targets to meet at any costs. It is necessary to grow a company by the very definition of what a business is, however, I believe we can limit our points of sales and still have a thriving international company. We are very happy to grow the company slowly and carefully so as not to compromise on anything we feel is important – our goal is to build a luxury brand which will stand the test of time, not simply to make a short-term profit. So we will sacrifice a certain amount of speed of expansion and profitability while still growing, in order to be able to reinvest our business and achieve economies of scale as we grow.

Finally Linda, I'd love to know which scents have sparked your imagination throughout your life and what unfulfilled dreams remain in your olfactory imagination?

My first proper 'grown-up' perfume was Madame Rochas in a tall crystal bottle. The perfume was the colour of Cognac and the overall look was so glamourous to me (aged ten) that it sat on my dressing table as the main focal point of my bedroom. It triggered my desire for perfume and over the years I have probably worn around 400 different fragrances. Diorella mixed with Eau Savage was my teenage years signature scent and the boys loved it. Then came First by Van Cleef & Arpels which reminds me so much of my first flat, first bed, and my own first pillow.

I have many ideas for perfumes all stored in my head. It is what I do and when a new oil comes my way, I more or less know what will become of it quite quickly. I love to look at the natural environment of a particular flower or resin to decide what will compliment and allow the perfume to sing in its natural harmony. I have travelled extensively in my life and lived in many different places including a number of years respectively in South America, the Middle East, Eastern Europe and Africa. I continue to enjoy travelling with my husband to the Middle East and Asia, as well as places of beauty closer to home. In each place, I have always tried to explore the local culture, cuisine, flora and fauna and this, I believe, will continue to be a source of inspiration well into the future.

THORSTEN BIEHL

Fragrance expert Thorsten Biehl on the art of perfumery, mass goods and personality.

Thorsten Biehl is a traveller. At the age of 16 he went to New York with his father, the renowned perfumer Henning Biehl, and this metropolis proved to be Thorsten Biehl's inspiration. It quite literally formed him. Open to learning, he enjoyed experiencing new cultures and went on to explore over 60 countries. His career path took him to Europe, South America and Asia, and then in 1999 back to his beloved New York. Founded in 2007 in Hamburg, his biehl.parfumkunstwerke company now has a base in Berlin and naturally, New York.

After a youth spent in Manhattan, Thorsten Biehl initially returned to Germany – to his birthplace in Holzminden in Lower Saxony. He embarked on a career as a fragrance expert in 1987 with one of the world's leading fragrance companies, now known as Symrise. The art of perfume sparked his imagination, and his passion prompted him to perfect his expertise in market positioning and development strategies for perfumes. He eventually became Marketing Director for International Fragrance Development in New York in 1999.

After gaining sufficient experience, he decided to take the plunge and launch into his new (ad)venture. He has successfully transformed an unusual concept into a workable reality reflecting his own life. The olfactory gallery he has since created has a resolutely international flavour. Six perfumers from five different countries have so far created luxury fragrances for Biehl and this is only the beginning of his journey as an independent entrepreneur. After cities like Los Angeles, Moscow, Rome and Zurich, biehl.parfumkunstwerke (which translates as Biehl Perfume works of art) are set for market launches in London, Dubai, Shanghai and Sao Paulo.

◯ Other people open a store. Unlike them, you talk of an 'olfactory gallery'. What precisely do you mean by that?

That's really quite simple: I understand my perfumes as works of art – so I open a gallery. For works of art, of course, a museum would also be a possibility. Yet unlike a museum, primarily intended to conserve, a gallery is a lively spot. Here people are actually living and things are constantly changing. My idea is to use this place to cultivate the art of perfume in an original way. And a gallery naturally gives you the opportunity to purchase a genuine work of art, or kunstwerk!

◯ So your perfumes are each unique?

Each bottle cannot be unique – but they all appear in limited editions. I truly do not offer concoctions for the masses. What I offer is a collection of truly exclusive fragrances composed by a small number of the finest and most respected perfumers in the world.

◯ How do you want to respond to growing demand with a scheme like this?

My perfumes stand for personality, which is not a mass product. I am also uncomprisingly behind the concept of perfume as a work of art. That means top quality in respect of the ingredients and the choice of perfumers. Even in future, therefore, my fragrances will only be available in limited editions. Yet we shall naturally be seeing additional biehl.parfumkunstwerke – new compositions and also new perfumes.

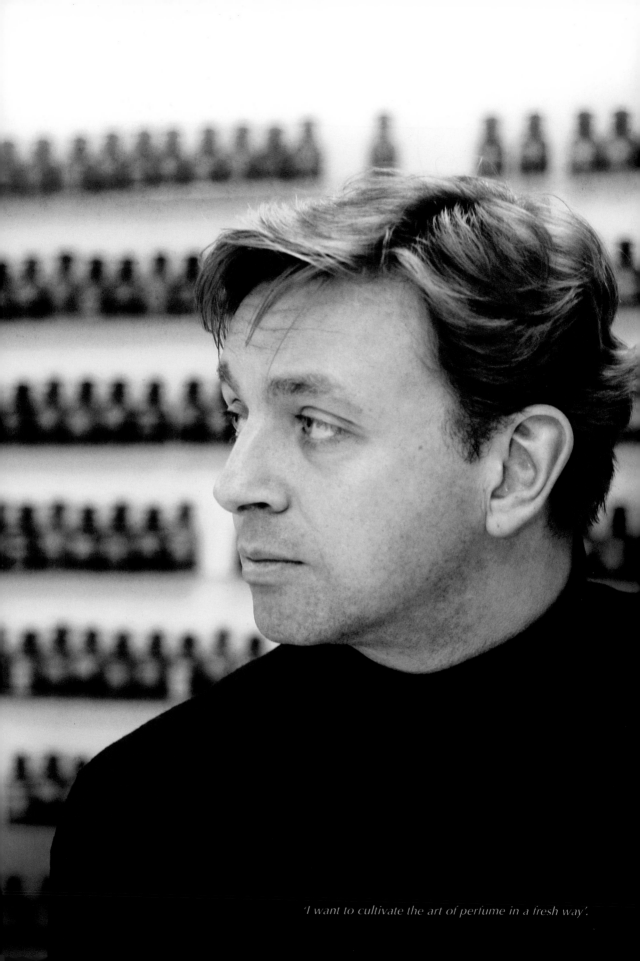

'I want to cultivate the art of perfume in a fresh way'.

Q How were you able to attract your present perfumers for biehl. parfumkunstwerke?

I have been developing fragrance concepts for international customers for nearly 20 years. Over that period I have naturally got to know numerous outstanding perfumers all over the world. My perfumers have simply been persuaded by my concept: total creative freedom. In creating perfumes, as a rule one, has to take into account many market pressures. What I seek and aim for is originality. These people have the most creative minds in the business; they are bold and passionate.

Q Yet your packaging and flacon design, by contrast, is extremely minimalist. Have you no misgivings that your products could be overlooked?

My collection is centered on the product and the artist. So I can do without fancy trimmings and outlandish flacon design. Less, but what is essential – that is what I aim for. I believe that the purism of the products will catch people's eye. I also carefully select the environment or, in other words, my sales partners. All this needs to match my brand concept. You will only find my parfumkunstwerke with real perfume enthusiasts, or with people who set the same store by quality and creativity as we do.

Q Like fashion, the world of fragrance is determined by trends. Do you track these with your products?

I naturally keep an eye on trends but trendy fragrances are not what I want to produce. Such products are transitory and leave no traces. Every year hundreds of new products arrive on the market, most of these being main stream. What's more, 97% of all perfumes launched do not survive a third year. By contrast, I regard the sustainability of a perfume creation as crucial. If you use a perfume, then you really want to live (with) this fragrance, not to see it disappear at once. And if I offer a perfume, I want it to make an impact and show the world its character. No, my fragrances cannot be trendy, although they may modern and contemporary.

biehl. parfumkunstwerke

gs01

biehl. parfumkunstwerke

mb01

biehl. parfumkunstwerke

al01

Q There are thousands of scents on the market. Why should a consumer opt for a biehl.parfumkunstwerke?

I am convinced that those who take the term 'individuality' seriously, and fill this with life – their own life! – will find that my products appeal to them, those are my customers. My products certainly bring along a lot of character. Yet at the same time they succeed perfectly in bringing out a human being's personality. I see my products as a means of self-expression, subtle and yet sovereign. For the same reason, incidentally, I am against the traditional division of perfumes for women and for men. I would perhaps recommend a specific perfume or orientation to a man or a woman, but I regard these categorisations as obsolete. I feel that every person needs to feel at ease with his or her perfume. After all, you do not let anything else get so close to you as a scent.

Q What inspires you personally?

I have travelled a great deal, and with passion, both on business and privately. Other countries, other cultures, repeatedly act as a stimulus for me. Then there are all the people that I encounter, their lives, their point of view... Really I am constantly hunting for fragrances and smells. Other people go about the world with open eyes, with me it's with an open nose, so to speak... Naturally I also let myself be inspired by art, by fashion, by design; the world is full of these things. Yet fragrances themselves – for me those are the greatest inspiration.

Q Which biehl. parfumkunstwerke do you use yourself?

I use several. Depending on my mood, it's the one that best expresses my attitude to life. I don't know whether I have a favourite. Each in its own distinctive way... I feel that all of the fragrances are equally successful. Otherwise I could not offer them to my customers.

We collect little fragments of life along our way and perfume is a wonderful way of conjuring memories of that journey. Smells lurk and hide in the recesses of our memory.

The study of raw materials revealed to me how powerful our olfactory memory can be. The whiff of a scented paper strip and a surge of emotion envelops you like a soft, scented cloud; like the scent of autumn rain that can hide in that strange synthetic molecule, isobutylquinolein. For me this scent conjures an image: of my father, the rain, soaking wet feet as I stood at the corner of the street and, in particular, the delicious smell of the waterproof mackintosh that he would slip over my shoulders.

There were thousands of molecules to master; an encyclopedia of emotions to digest. It all made my head spin as a 17 year old! Opting for creative freedom has allowed me to follow my desires. I think what sets me apart is my independent spirit. I choose to work away from large groups, off the beaten track. This freedom steers me away from the typical reflexes of a perfumer and away from current trends.

Q How challenging is it to work on fragrances that are far removed from things you know? Is it something you find exciting and enjoyable or do you feel it distorts your sense of reality?

Perfume needs to have meaning. Lots of perfumes leave me totally indifferent; like watching a film with no plot. You leave the cinema feeling slightly empty. You just spray those kinds of perfume on without thinking, out of habit. I don't like vague or blurred perfumes that say nothing, nor do I like overtly primary notes. I like perfumes to be simply but precisely drawn allowing for nuance and charm. It's important to stop and smell the roses, notice things, where others just run on by.

I refuse to be a slave to the latest perfume trends. I love exploring and inventing new territory, working against the grain - as long as there is a genuine idea behind it all and it's coherent, authentic and someone has experienced it.

OLIVIA GIACOBETTI

Q Your creations are admired for their delicacy, mystery and serenity. Would you say these qualities are a reaction to experiences you have lived through?

I invest a lot of myself because a perfume devoid of emotion is devoid of meaning to me. When I was starting out, I found the perfumes at the time tended to be too heavy, too stuffy and old-fashioned. Perfume was and is a living language to me. I dreamed of fig trees, fresh water, sun dried linen... I wanted to narrate scented stories; to capture a moment, a sensation; the atmosphere of a gypsy circus, or the mood of city; the smell of a beach or a fire.

Q What kind of childhood, what memories do creators draw their inspiration from?

Olfactory memory is subjective. How necessary is other people's recognition or praise to you? Is it important for your perfumes to have an effect on strangers?

I never feel I have entirely finished a creation. It's often the brand I am creating a fragrance for or the market's own limitations which dictate my creative boundaries. During the whole creative process I tend to steer clear of passing criticism so as not to get distracted.

Above all, I need to believe in what I am doing. Of course I need other's opinions but shyness dictates that the closer a fragrance is to me, the more I doubt people will like it. I prefer to rely on the opinions and reactions of those close to me, I find they are much better reference points.

Above and beyond commercial success, the greatest compliment is when someone reacts emotionally to my perfumes. I remember a child sat next to me once in a garden and turned to me and said: "you smell nice, like sunshine". I was wearing Premier Figuier that I'd created for L'Artisan Parfumeur at the time. This kind of thing spurs me on and keeps any professional doubt at bay for a while.

I have never gone for a project for its size, importance or power of distribution. My perfume creations are confidential; I prefer to practice invention and this always takes longer.

In recent years we have seen a lot of changes in the fragrance industry - some very controversial as they ban or restrict the use of certain materials. Do you see this as inevitably negative, given that many classic fragrances now have to be either 'reworked' or discontinued, or do you feel there is room for new methods and innovation to replicate these scents?

Perfume industry regulations have become increasingly tough. No one can deny that the banning of certain raw materials is proving to be like a death sentence for some great perfumes out there. Nothing can perfectly replace certain components. You can substitute or disguise, but the result will never be the same. Can you replace butter with low

fat spread or oil? Gourmet chefs will tell you no. The composition of modern day perfumes is a whole different debate. Unfortunately, the manufacturers of raw materials tend to focus their investment on maintaining existing materials, rather than innovation into new ones. This means new molecules are sparse. If more materials are to disappear? I'm not sure which one I would miss the most. All of them!

It's so hard to live without certain materials; lots of them yield great things and others can be so discreet that they will no doubt be discontinued at some point. The more you 'sanitise' the overall picture - remove some yellow here, some red there- the canvas will begin to look a little lackluster and homogeneous. We should stay optimistic though. Let's not forget that with very few musical notes to play with we've still managed to go from Bach to the Rolling Stones…

Q Which defining moment sealed your destiny as a perfumer? Is there a perfume that stops you in your tracks? Can you tell us your all time most precious scents or fragrances?

I was young when I decided I wanted to work in this business. I was ten, sitting in the cinema watching Le Sauvage (The Wild One) by Jean-Paul Rappeneau and was struck by the island that featured the workshop and the fragrance strips… I became obsessed with becoming a perfumer and I have never wanted to do anything else since. Perfumes that have touched me deeply are Tabu by Dana, Youth Dew, Cabochard… Childhood memories! A fragrance that has stayed with me for over 30 years is Kiehl's Musk that my father brought back from New York for my sister. I pinched a few drops and it remains for me the most seductive fragrance ever, it reminds me of America and is always with me. I also fell in love with Féminité du Bois by Serge Lutens, with its natural wood, so whole, elegant, warm and troubling. It's like I've always known it and I can't do without it. I love wood in all its forms: blond or black; damp or scorched; dry or buttery; soft or ambiguous; on a man or a woman.

Q Do you find yourself analysing smells and scents everywhere you go? I would imagine you are constantly absorbing and computing information that

can only enrich your palette of ideas and olfactory landscapes in your mind?

True! I think it's the case for all perfumers. Everywhere I go, I steal, collect, pick up and bring things back, be it a flower, a piece of burned wood, a leaf or a pebble. In Mali I broke bits of bark off yellow wood that smelled of quinces, I picked up cooked rice grains and pieces of burned string. In Japan, I discovered a soft rubber that smelled of Christmas, puffed rice and neon pink ribbons that smelled of plastic dolls. I have stolen incense from a Malaysian temple so as never to forget its scent. In Mexico I was struck by the smell of floating wood, fresh cactus and black corn… Cities fascinate me; they're like scented kaleidoscopes, an explosion of smells.

Istanbul smells of roses and dust; New York of clean laundry, Kraft cream cheese and cinnamon; Paris of static electricity, fresh bread and wet pavements; Katmandu smells of dry wood and cucumber; Tokyo of toast or something that's been grilled, metal and plastic. Attention to detail is what matters. I've been to the end of the world on my quests but have also found inspiration fetching bread from the corner shop!

Q How do you feel about the perfume business now and what do you think the future holds for us in that respect?

Things change. A perfume you've worn all your life can suddenly seem so old-fashioned. We've lost our sense of loyalty, we've become flighty, bulimic; we change our minds at the drop of a hat and get bored… The perfume industry is drowning in this universal hotpot as it tries to please all of the people. Perfume isn't Coca-Cola you know! We're at that stage where perfumes come and go within months, all merging into each other. Most of the big brands try to re-establish an element of prestige by creating private collections. They're harking back to old style luxury and revisiting classic scents like Colognes, chyprés, amber, leather, tobacco… There has to be some sort of fall-out from this loss of identity. Maybe something creative will come to pass where least expected…

Q Would you say you are always completely satisfied with every one of your creations and which makes you the most proud?

My character dictates that I can never actually be proud, but I do derive pleasure from creating what I love. Yet when I've finished creating a fragrance, it's gone. It's living out adventures on other people's skin and I forget it. I rediscover it through others when they wear it but I try to keep my distance for fear of finding fault in it. Therefore, I choose to look to the future, to everything I have yet to achieve. I love Premier Figuier because that's my tree, the tree that represents my childhood and the first scent to use fig as its central note. It set a fragrance trend and ever since little fig trees have sprouted up everywhere. I wear l'Ether by Iunx; it's like a soft cloud of incense resin and I find it very calming.

Q How does perfume makes you tick?

Perfume is all encompassing and magical. How incredible to think that this invisible cloak can wrap itself around us, unlock our emotions and hold us spellbound with the stories it unfolds.

Perfume is a passion for me. I love the poetry that surrounds the world of smells. I love the subtlety and depth of its language, an almost 'animal' ability to tap into our emotions. Perfume is like a language of symbols that speaks to our subconscious. Our sense of smell is the only one to transmit information directly to our emotional brain – analysing later. Our olfactory memory is indelible which is very troubling because we can forget a face, a voice even, but never a smell.

Q Finally Olivia, what does the future holds for us as your fans?

Lots of things! I'm lucky to have lots of different projects on the go. I've just finished a piece of work that is 100% natural, the result is really interesting, like a fountain of truth with surprising notes within it. The rest is still confidential. Iunx is my playground into which I invest all that I love. The brand will evolve nice and slowly and that's the way it should be.

Q Geza Schoen, your fragrance portfolio is eclectic and innovative encompassing a range of different styles and brands. You have carved yourself a great career and reputation and have tended to shun mainstream projects. Have you always naturally set yourself apart or has this gradually developed as a result of disappointing experiences and disillusionment with the perfume business?

Phew, that is a very complex matter. I was dragged through museums and art galleries from day one by my father who is an art enthusiast. Making things on my own, but differently, became somewhat standard for me. Furthermore, the industry makes it really easy for us, just look at what they are doing. The numerous launches bamboozle loyal fans of a brand and, in addition, all big brands have a very strong pattern they think they need to follow – they just don't dare enough. At the end of the day they forget the most important thing: a luxurious product like an expensive perfume needs a soul, or at least a story, wrapped around it. The Beautiful Mind series is my automatic reaction to the unacceptable nonsense ever since certain celebrities made their appearance in fragrance. I just thought "enough is enough", let's celebrate someone with a real human skill.

Q The perfume business is complex, not to mention a money spinner, for most brands and normally requires important marketing investment and communication. Escentric Molecule and your collaboration flipped things around didn't it? It has smashed all expectations despite its confidential almost underground beginnings. Did you have any idea how receptive your audience would be to this ground breaking approach and scent?

No, not at all. I knew people were bored beyond belief, but that was easy to tell, I have been watching the perfume market now for almost 30 years and the fragrance world has certainly lost its magic of originality. Corporations have a marketing plan to fulfill – we don't do that. Our scents market themselves by smelling different but good. We are lucky that we managed to hit a nerve with the consumer. Clients all come back to

us with the same feedback: they have never worn such an attention grabbing scent where people keep asking them what they are wearing. They feel flattered. That is all rather fabulous.

🔲 Have you ever witnessed the effect Molecule 01 has on people first hand? I never quite believed it until my fiancé tried it to astonishing effect! Strangers, friends, colleagues – everyone compliments him on it. Needless to say he won't wear anything else ever again now... Did you envisage this happening with your knowledge of the molecule Iso E Super being what it was?

This was honestly never my plan! I have been aware since 1991 of the effect the molecule can have on its own but I had envisioned mol01 to be for (perfume) freaks, the ones who wanted to create an aura, rather than wear a perfume. And less seems to be more! Our recipe for success is actually quite simple: smell different but desirable.

🔲 The main companies developing synthetics and new molecules are constantly innovating and perfecting these compounds. What would be your ideal synthetic molecule to be created at some point in the future?

In terms of sheer beauty we won't see it, it is all there already. We are constantly loosing raw materials – that is more of a worry for me. We have reached a stage where the lobbying body for IFRA and eco-press is so huge that perfume producing companies will eliminate ingredients of their own volition just to be on the safe side. It's a pathetic state of affairs. Our industry is spineless and seems incapable to hold this off. I think we are much likelier to see new cuts of certain naturals which can make a difference to a perfume creation.

Coming back to your question, it is hard to imagine new olfactory features in a molecule if you look at what already exists. We don't need the 86th different sandalwood ingredient or another musk. The industry hasn't exploited any more natural raw materials because it has become increasingly more expensive to even launch new chemical materials to better them.

GEZA SCHOEN

Q You have worked with Abroxan, the synthetic Ambergris note. If budget and supply were not an issue would you favour the synthetic or natural raw material for a creation, and can you explain the differences in working with each?

Well of course I would always favour the natural for its complexity. Imagine being able to extract natural ambroxan from real ambergris – that would be hideously expensive!

In general we have to come away from the idea that natural is always 'good' and chemicals are all 'bad'. It does not really matter what origin a material has, as long as it works. Most chemicals are less harmful than natural ingredients which might contain traces of molecules leading them to be prohibited, or at least restricted, in their usage. A perfume that's only composed of naturals would smell awful on your skin as at some point, these naturals leave a fatty unpleasant odour. That said, a perfume only composed of chemicals has no soul and would smell odd too. Unless of course you happen to bump into mol01, that is different as the ingredient is omnipotent.

Q Are you quite secretive about your work or do you like to share aspects of your work in progress?

I have no problem sharing my work; I have learned in the past that only the less creative need to keep their achievements to themselves so that at least they can keep that little bit of difference. If you don't progress and come up with creative solutions all the time you might as well start doing something else. There are reported incidents of perfumers attacking each other over formulas, or laboratories being contaminated with some disgusting smell so that other people passing by wouldn't get a whiff of the heavenly concoction under creation. In that particular case the actual result in the market was pathetic and the fragrance is no longer with us. The problem is the money spinning side of the industry treat their perfumers like battery hens – well paid but with no freedom to create due to cost restrictions and so called guidelines. When working on a personal project, raw material cost is never an issue – it's the only way to not restrict yourself creatively from the start.

Q You obviously love the emotional response your fragrances elicit but would you, or do you, derive as much pleasure from your fragrances if they only pleased you and the person most important to you? Is it vital for a perfumer's creations to live and be loved through others – to be recognized – or is that just the icing on the cake?

Excellent question. I need another cup of tea. I always loved the moment when my friends or my girlfriend would only wear a particular perfume I gave them. As a perfumer you need to learn to play a highly charged political game. Imagine you as a team get a briefing for the next Gucci-Armani-Versace. Wouldn't you want to win this over one of your colleagues? Nowadays you need to come up with the goods or face being being kicked out at some point and I guess this is fair enough given the financial circumstamces even creative companies live under. You need to win projects otherwise your status is in jeopardy. It did change for me a little bit after I won my first commercial fine fragrance in 1994. It was a bit like "oh, it really works – now I want more".

Q Which moment in your life do you think defined your destiny as a perfumer? Is there a perfume that can literally stop you in your tracks and bring tears to your eyes or give you goose pimples just from one sniff? Or can you tell us your all time most precious scent memories?

There are moments which are loaded with molecules you really do want to smell and others you would love to avoid as they really bring you back to experiences. We cannot escape the strong emotional implication past memories have had, and will continue to evoke, forever more. This is mesmerising; no other sense is capable of such a strong impact. Some moments were very special in an olfactory sense, like when I visited Hasslauer in the 1990s in Paris. It was the only house manufacturing real ambergris and there was one room where they stored different pieces of the real stuff. They led me into this room and I nearly fainted it was so beautiful and intense, probably the closest to what we would imagine Jean-Baptiste Grenouille's juice would do! (the

lead protagonist in the novel Perfume by Patrick Süskind). Most scented memories will stay with me as a kind of a personal diary.

Q Which fragrances have touched you in your life? Was your reaction due to the person wearing it or was it the time and place or all of these and more?

There are definitely some cool fragrances around. Chanel19 was the first one which caught me; a friend of my parents wore this, she had leather gloves and the scent would stick to the gloves forming this incredible aroma with the leather and her skin. I worked this impression into a fragrance later. You can buy it but I am not allowed to tell you which brand it was created for. Several others I love include Alliage, Jules, Anaïs Anaïs, Halston z14, Eau Sauvage, Giorgio, Féminité du Bois, Antaeus – most of these are older ones or classics, I don't care too much for the fragrances launched over the past 10-15 years... Ah! Comme2 (for Comme des Garçons) by my friend Mark Buxton is exceptional!

Q Do you find yourself analysing smells and scents everywhere you go? I would imagine you are constantly absorbing and computing information that can only enrich your palette of ideas and olfactory landscapes in your mind?

Yes. Good fun! I sometimes wish I could smell less analytically and be more generally perceptive if that makes sense.

Q How do you feel about the perfume business now and what do you think the future holds for us in that respect?

I feel great about the perfume business. We have been able to add our personal chapter to it and we have fans worldwide reporting that we have given them something they have been looking for all their life. That is exactly what we do: lifetime scents.

Q If there were a dream perfume collaboration you could choose who would it be with?

Maradona

Q Would you say you are always completely satisfied with every one of your creations, and which makes you the most proud?

Noooooo, I am not always satisfied, that is impossible. I think escentric01 is very close to my understanding of perfumery: fresh, spicy, transparent, woody, balsamic, musky, sexy.

Q As a life-long perfume lover, obsessed with the effect perfume can have on me and people around me, I am very interested to know what it is about perfume that speaks to you and makes you tick?

I grew up in the garden of my grandparents with pear trees and chickens running around, Grandma cooking food and making marmalade. There was room for the senses to develop. Perfume is probably the most abstract thing you could create. Unless you are in it, you are miles away from doing something remotely similar. We can all play a few notes on a piano, we can all paint a picture or decide how our bedroom should look but perfume has an aura of magic around it you cannot imagine. I guess it had the biggest wow factor around it, which is why I fell for it.

Q Finally Geza, I am curious to know what the future holds for us as your fans?

Ooooohhhhhh, escentric03 and molecule03 this autumn. And it looks like I have found a second person to feature the next edition of The Beautiful Mind series, can't say more yet... sorry.

123
456
789

PERFUME – THE FUTURE

A MODERN APPROACH

We live in the age of 'Me'. From our iPhone playlists to our blogs and our tweets, our custom-created Nike trainers to our coffee orders, we long to look, to be – and most definitely to smell – different from everyone else.

There is a new kind of perfume-lover emerging: the fragrance individualist. Instead of splashing on a bestselling fragrance, however beautiful, which everyone can identify, this fragrance individualist longs for a little more mystery. Not, "oh, you're wearing Jennifer Lopez/Britney/Kate Moss." But "oh, what's that wonderful scent you have on…?" How we love our fragrance secrets. Few understood that better than Estée Lauder who wafted through life on a cloud of the unique scent she had hoped to keep for herself, until persuaded otherwise by women who implored her to reveal its identity. Thus, Private Collection – her own opulent floral – was shared with the world, but more of that anon. The vast majority of fragrance may still be bought in giant marbled beauty halls (and, speaking realistically, Duty Free), but there is something very special about sleuthing out a scent that's so precious, unique and different that your best friend has never even heard of it. Our yearning to dab on something unique is bringing about a subtle shift in the scent world…

Take Frederic Malle, whose 'light bulb' moment was to offer free rein to some of the 20th century's greatest noses to create their ultimate perfume under the Editions de Parfums imprint. (And for the first time to give credit where it's due, emblazoning the creator's name on the bottle.) Without Malle, fragranceaholics would have been deprived of: Ralf Schweiger's Lipstick Rose with its violet whispers of mummy's handbag; Dominic Ropion's Vetiver Extraordinaire, a quintet of woody notes with a forest-floor dampness; or Bigarade Concentrée by Jean-Claude Ellena - his whoosh of marmalade-bitter oranges and hesperidic freshness is a quintessential Cologne to be applied liberally and adored by women and men. "I decided to bring perfumers into the sunlight and 'publish' their personal and unique creations. The well-known saying: 'Perfumer, your name is nobody' is no longer true," observed Malle.

More recently, stepping into the sunlight (and spotlight) to tease our senses has been Francis Kurkdjian. Creator of the blockbuster men's fragrance Le Male for Jean-Paul Gaultier, he quit his role at one of the world's biggest fragrance houses to open a 'custom fragrance' atelier - and latterly Maison Francis Kurkdjian, offering his non-bespoke fragrance concepts on the Rue d'Alger in Paris.

Today, both Malle's and Kurkdjian's creations can be enjoyed outside Paris, too. Department stores keen not to let sales slip through their fingers have begun to create boutiques within a store for these ground breaking perfumers. Look out too for labels like LeLabo, with its mission statement: 'To create ten exceptional fragrances, with no eye on costs and one goal – to create a sensory shock as soon as you open the bottle.' Also increasingly on the global radar is a fragrance house by the name of by Kilian founded by Kilian Hennessy, grandson of the LVMH luxury groups founder and heir to the Hennessy cognac business. His leitmotif in every scent features the rich undertones of the wood from – what else? – cognac barrels.

Close to home, waving the Union Jack for perfume creativity and independence are talented British noses Linda Pilkington (whose postage-stamp of a boutique in Bond Street's Royal Arcade is worthy of a lazy, sense-drenching hour or two), and Lyn Harris (who, intriguingly, is now staging a reverse-invasion of Paris with her perfect, airy Colognes). Let's not forget professeur de parfums Roja Dove, who (after 25 years selling other people's fragrances) has created a trio of his own, with enticingly wicked names like Scandal, Unspoken and Enslaved - all showcased in his Moroccan-inspired, lacquered-black perfume kasbah in Harrods.

First the good news: no jet-lag, no expensive air fares or Eurostar tickets required for our 'fix'. Then, just the merest twinge of regret: the fragrant trophy, a bit like an olfactory passport stamp, can no longer be selfishly kept to ourselves. So today we can breathe in the precious frankincense smokiness of Amouage without need to holiday in the sun-drenched Sultanate of Oman. Is Annick Goutal's zesty Eau Hadrien any less crisply wonderful just because

millions of women zingalong with it, today? Don't we love Santa Maria Novella's Melograno with its tart pomegranate tang, just as much even though we no longer require a foray to Florence to find it? A rose (fragrance) in any other city will still smell as sweet. (Ditto iris, jasmine, lilac, orange blossom...)

There's one hidden bonus of this renaissance of the perfumer's art: with money no object in the creation of many of these more exclusive niche fragrances, they tend to feature higher proportions of natural ingredients. In contrast to synthetic ingredients, which tend to develop in a predictable way on the skin, these natural elements are subtly adjusted by our body chemistry. So when applied to the body and skin-warmed, each scent becomes as individual as handwriting.

What's interesting meanwhile is how this 'boutique' fragrance trend has started to influence the mainstream. In an echo of Frederic Malle, Chanel not long ago gave legendary nose Jacques Polge this chance. The result is Les Exclusifs which includes No18 – named after the mansion on Place Vendôme that Coco Chanel could see from her Ritz balcony during the war – it swirls sparklingly around a sweet heart of ambrette from the hibiscus flower. 28 La Pausa has the signature velvety powder of precious iris. More recently Sycomore, Polge's reprise of a 78 year old smoky vetiver scent from the archives has been added to Les Exclusifs collection. It was Chanel's own dream of the perfect woody, no-frills fragrance – it is suddenly, perfectly 'now'.

So if you've ever felt that perfume had dumbed-down, the tide has just turned. Today, anyone who longs to express their individuality through their choice of scent has an almost bewildering and utterly bewitching range of cult scent options. You won't find them in Duty Free or stumble upon them when buying toothpaste – and they're all the more special for that. They're all about you. And all about me. And most especially, all about the talented elite of perfumers, creating eaux and essences with nothing in mind but to delight our senses.

Vive l'indépendence…!
Josephine Fairley

THE FUTURE OF SCENT

You have to wonder what it would have been like to have stood on the edge of 1882 and been granted a vision of the future of perfume.

It was the year perfume joined music, painting and literature and became an art. In 1875, the British chemist William Henry Perkin had synthesised the molecule coumarin. Now, seven years later, the perfumer Paul Parquet would put it into a perfume that the house of Houbigant called Fougère Royale. In an instant, perfume freed itself from natural materials, its artisans suddenly transformed into artists. Art is artificial in the best sense: It is the result of a mind, an artistic vision, a will that says, "I will make you experience X." Parquet made you experience Fougère Royale, and he did it on his own terms.

A new artistic medium was created. It's not every day this happens.

The synthetics, the marvelous creations, had just begun to make their appearance. In 1889 the American student Francis Dodge synthesised citronellal (fresh lemon, rose) and Ferdinand Tiemann figured out how to extract alpha- and beta-ionones (violets, iris root). Baur, who had been working on trinitrotoluene (TNT), exploded perfumery in 1888 by synthesising the first nitrated musks. In a single year, 1879, heliotropin and vanillin were both smelted, making Guerlain's pre-war masterpieces possible.

The artists seized these machines and ran with them. L.T. Piver took the methyl salicylate Darzens had discovered in 1896 and launched Trèfle Incarnat in 1907. François Coty put out Origan in 1910, Jacques Guerlain l'Heure Bleue and Houbigant's Quelques Fleurs came in 1912 and 1913. And eight years later Ernest Beaux threw fistfuls of glittering synthesised aldehydes into Chanel No5 like silver acrylic confetti cloaking a beautiful woman. No one had ever seen anything like it because no one ever could have.

We are continually waking up in the future. You can't imagine it until it appears. Unless you're the person creating it, of course. Edmond Roudnitska created it in 1964 with Eau Sauvage by brilliantly overdosing a molecule called methyl dihydrojasmonate (sold under the trade name Hedione) that had been synthesised by Firmenich two years earlier. Pierre Wargnye, Jacques Cavallier and Olivier Cresp built futures and watched as we walked into them: Drakkar Noir, l'Eau d'Issey, Angel. (Dihydromyrcenol, Calone, and ethyl maltol, brilliantly used to create innovative visions of new works of art.) Le Feu and hydroxy butyl thiazol. Gucci Rush and lactones. I could go on and on. If you are ever tempted to think you've seen everything, just wait.

The future of perfume has always been the progression of the creative imagination using progressing materials. Perhaps architecture is the best analogy here. Baked earth was the revolution millennia ago. Super light/strong metal alloys are the revolution today. Combine the materials with the mind that sees the way to use them, and that is the building you will see tomorrow. The perfumers who create the future are the perfumers who think. Dihydromyrcenol had come to define the scent of laundry detergents by the 1970s, and Pierre Wargnye put it in Drakkar Noir in the 1980s, not because of this but because it had also come, psychologically, to define the scent of 'clean'.

The future has always had its discontented – generally they are the religious – and we shouldn't be surprised that this is exactly the situation with perfume. The all-natural fundamentalists with their laws of olfactory kashrut. They generate the usual tortured reasoning for tarring synthetics as trefe. This is as rational as refusing to look at a painting done in acrylics. But irrationality is a necessary component of fanaticism.

But the damage has actually been done by the marketers, of course. To marketers, the future is the enemy. You can't predict it. It's difficult to commodify. And it's extremely difficult to write ad copy for something that by definition defies ad copy. True novelty is initially indescribable. The marketers pay lip service: half-hypocritical, half-naïve-to the all-natural theology that dislikes the materials that permit the future, because that theology speaks to the lowest common denominator.

It's a complete lie, of course, but that's beside the point. The point is what sells. The marketers treat consumers like idiots because many of them are idiots.

I would argue that those are the ones who aren't going to read anything anyway. They'll look at the pretty girl in the ad, the chrome-plated brand and the other shiny baubles, and obediently get out their credit cards. Those at the other end of the spectrum will practice their religion and deprive themselves, self-righteous and blind, of the latest work of genius. As for them, they're not going to buy the marketers' stuff anyway.

That leaves clients who know something about this art form. Speak to them. They will read. And they will ignore the laws of kashrut. They will talk about your new perfume with interest, and they will want to understand the new material inside it. (Have you heard? A molecule that smells of rhubarb fruit with a bitter tang. Paving tar with a floral angle. No! Who's the perfumer? Ah, I loved his latest. I can't wait to smell his latest work.)

That's the future. Sephora, Macy's and Saks as marvelous art galleries where you can actually afford the works of art offered to delight or stun, scare or mesmerize you. The great collectors of paintings are those who, somehow, see today on the canvas what the artist saw last year and what the rest of us will see in a decade. "What an age is like," wrote W.H. Auden, "is never what it thinks it is, which is why the best art of any period, the art which the future realises to be the product of its time, is usually rather disliked when it appears."

The future of perfume is J'adore, an instant commercial success, and Le Feu, an instant commercial failure. Both will guide creations still downstream from us, and if we'll never know what will sell, we'll also never know what we will consider great, regardless of its box office.

I'm writing this on a Wednesday. This Friday I'm invited by Symrise to a lunch celebrating the launch of their latest captive, Ambrocenide®. None of the traditional Firmenich secretive paranoia here – the furtive, myopic, suffocating fear with which IFF and Givaudan surround their captives. Hell, Symrise is throwing a party for the thing. They've got it completely right, of course. It's the only logical way to introduce a new synthetic. If the client isn't an idiot, she'll want to know. She'll be eager to smell where the artists, Vasnier, Bijaoui, Kurkdjian, Laurent, will be taking us. It's a new world, and with little Ambrocenide it has just become newer. Happy Birthday, baby. I'm looking forward to the lunch, and I'm eager to smell the future. Who knows what will happen.

Chandler Burr

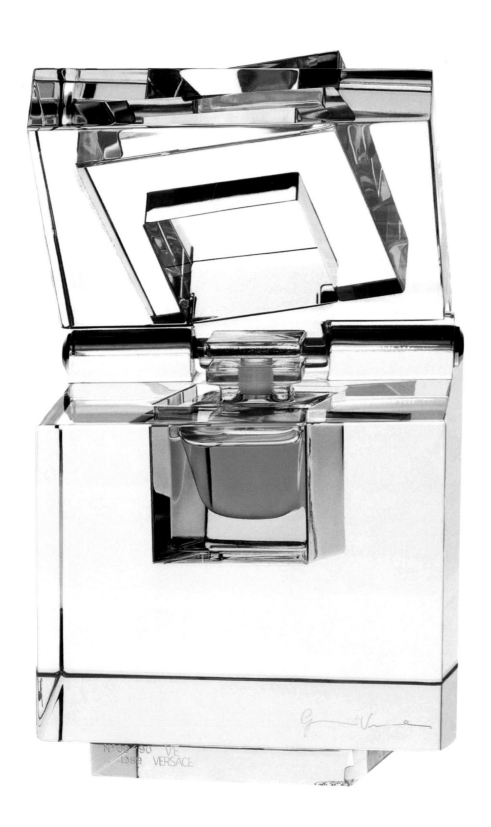

N° 00790 V/E
1989 VERSACE

I have always said that I have lived the life I was born to lead. At some specific long lost moment a fragrant molecule entered my being and I was forever changed, my destiny was forged, its path galvanised. There was no other path to tread than that of perfumery, and along its colourful brick-road I have encountered the work of mighty geniuses who allow their creativity to become part of our core, our being, our ID – as it stops us dead in our tracks, brings tears to our eyes or smiles to our faces. How can anyone not love perfumery?

I hope you have enjoyed this book and your journey through the diversity of styles which make up modern perfumery. It is interesting to note how often each brand started in a very small way, each one inspiring a trend or giving another the courage to try. At their helm were anonymous people who had a belief, a quest for perfection and a desire to create something new, often groundbreaking – whose echo still resonates today like the aftershock from a scented bomb.

When Pierre-François-Pascal Guerlain penned his first formula on the 10th August 1828 he could not possibly have conceived that five generations of his family would be perfumers. I always remember Jean-Paul Guerlain saying, when I worked at Guerlain, that he was luckier than most perfumers as he had over a hundred and seventy years of know-how.

So maybe the ancient Egyptians had it right in their belief that perfume has the ability to make us immortal. As we breathe in a scent and appreciate its gift to revive memories; as each perfumer learns their craft and passes it on to the next generation, a little bit of that ancient, innate knowledge must be lurking in each precious bottle. And it is brought to life so beautifully in this book as we explore the stories of the houses and some of the perfumers who shape our world today – and maybe it will even inspire a perfumer of tomorrow.

I am so pleased to have played my part in this olfactory compendium, which would not have come about without the foresight and passion of Anton Mossa and Nathalie Grainger from Quintessentially. The beauty of this pathway is that I not only get to smell incredible works of art, but also I meet wonderful new friends as I walk to my own olfactory Oz.

Summary

ACKNOWLEDGEMENTS

Firstly gratitude to the Quintessentially Publishing team who have become friends: Liam Wholey who offered the opportunity in the first place and whose faith never wavered; Managing Director, Edward Rodwell for his drive, energy, understanding of the project and utter dedication; Anton Mossa for the original idea of the book, his encouragement and personal guidance; Eleanor Horsey for the professionalism, perseverance and elegance in all her work and communication; Christopher Rayner for his advice, commercial expertise and loyalty; Lois Crompton for her sunny personality, objectivity and for knowing what to do; Barry Lynch and Russell Bryan for their sense of humour and friendship.

Thank you to our Design team, Leanne Simpson and the talented Marijus Burokas for his patience, vision and passionate creativity. Our editorial team, in particular Carol Krosnar for her painstaking attention to detail and her valuable time, Trevor Lewis for his assistance and expertise and to our external journalists and editors: Josephine Fairley, Vicci Bentley, Jo Glanville-Blackburn, Christopher Stocks, Chandler Burr and of course, Roja Dove, our Creative Director for his great generosity, insight, friendship and kindness. Appreciation to Geza Schoen, Camille Goutal, Isabelle Doyen, Bertrand Duchaufour, Linda Pilkington, Olivia Giacobetti, Clive Christian, Jean-François Latty, Paul White, Thorsten Biehl, Catherine Bossom, Jeff Lounds and Tim Blanks, Jamie Kelly, Emily Maben, Rebecca Pantling and the team at Senteurs d'Ailleurs in Brussels.

Special thanks and recognition must go to Charlotte McCarthy, Tom Stephan, Eric Meilhoc, Maria Pajares, Jo Tutchener, Michael Williamson, Cynthia Olson, Trudi Collister, Robert Gorman and Lourdes Santin for helping us to get in touch with the right people and being so generous. Lastly thank you so much to Paul Raeside and the Baccarat Heritage collection for the amazing photography offered and supplied.

On a personal note great thanks and love go to Jane, Dan and Lucy for their encouragement and finally, my parents, sister Juliet and Stuart for their unconditional love.

DIRECTORY

Zero Otto Srl
Via Mercantini 12
63039 San Benedetto del Tr. (AP)
Italy
info@zero-otto.com
www.zero-otto.com

ACQUA
DI
PARMA

Marble Arch House
66-68 Seymour Street
London, W1H 5AF
England
Tel: +44 1932 233 861
www.acquadiparma.com

14 Lowndes Street
London, SW1X 9EX
England
michyla@amouage.com, joyce@amouage.com
www.amouage.com

ANNICK GOUTAL
PARIS

Harrods
87–135 Brompton Road
London, SW1X 7XL
England
Tel: +44 207 730 1234
www.harrods.com

www.mirani.com
USA
Tel: +1 917 348 3636

73 Grosvenor Street
London, W1K 3BQ
England
Tel: +44 870 034 2566

Biehl
Parfumkunstwerke

Borsigstr. 8
d-10115
Berlin, Germany
Tel: +49 030 2758 1077
office@biehl-parfum.com
www.biehl-parfum.com

BVLGARI

Harrods
87–135 Brompton Road
London, SW1X 7XL
England
Tel: +44 207 730 1234
www.harrods.com

CALYX

73 Grosvenor Street
London, W1K 3BQ
England
Tel: +44 870 034 2566

ChristianDior

Tel: +44 207 216 0216
www.dior.com

56 Haymarket
London, SW1Y 4RN
England
Tel: +44 207 839 3434
customerservice@clive.com
www.clive.com

CLIVE CHRISTIAN
THE WORLDS MOST EXPENSIVE PERFUME

COMME des GARÇONS
*

16 Place Vendôme
75011 Paris
France
Tel: +33 1 47 03 60 86
parfum@comme-des-garcons.com
www.doverstreetmarket.com

DONNAKARAN
THE FRAGRANCE COLLECTION

73 Grosvenor Street
London, W1K 3BQ
England
Tel: +44 870 034 2566

Ebullience

Ebullience Perfume Company
222 North Columbus Avenue #1009
Chicago, IL 60601
USA
Tel: +1 312 339 4165
www.ebullienceperfume.com

escentric molecules

Lins House
38 Roseberry Avenue
London, EC1R 4RN
England
Tel: Jeff +44 7880 746 289
David +44 7787 500 729
jeff@thiscompany.org, david@thiscompany.org
www.escentric.com

GROSSMITH
LONDON

6 Deanery Street
London, W1K 1BA
England
Tel: +44 207 355 0355
Enquiries@GrossmithLondon.com
www.grossmithlondon.com

GUERLAIN

Tel: +44 1932 233 887

HERMÈS

Harrods
87–135 Brompton Road
London, SW1X 7XL
England
Tel: +44 207 730 1234

868 Post Street
San Francisco
CA 94109
USA
Tel: +1 415 928 5661
www.infiore.net

JEAN-CHARLES BROSSEAU

129, avenue Daumesnil
75012 Paris
France
Tel: +33 1 53 33 82 00
www.jcbrosseau.com

Jo MALONE
LONDON

Tel: +44 870 034 2411
info@jomalone.com
www.jomalone.com

L'Artisan Parfumeur
PARIS

www.artisanparfumeur.com

Maison Dorin
Museum
20, Rue Labélonye
78400 Chatou
France
Tel: + 33 1 30 15 40 40
www.maison-dorin.com

Miller Harris
PERFUMER · LONDON

21 Bruton Street
London, W1J 6QD
England
Tel: +44 207 629 7750
info@millerharris.com
www.millerharris.com

---

narciso rodriguez

Harrods
87–135 Brompton Road
London, SW1X 7XL
England
Tel: +44 207 730 1234

ORMONDE JAYNE

London Perfumery

12 The Royal Arcade
28 Old Bond Street
London, W1S 4SL
England
Tel: +44 207 499 1100
sales@ormondejayne.com
www.ormondejayne.com

By appointment to
HRH The Duke of Edinburgh
Manufacturers of Toilet Requisites
Penhaligon's Limited London

By appointment to
HRH The Prince of Wales
Manufacturers of Toilet Requisites
Penhaligon's Limited London

PENHALIGON'S

LONDON

Dragoon House
37-39 Artillery Lane
London, E1 7LP
England
Tel: +44 800 716 108
www.penhaligons.com

PRO
FVMVM
ROMA

Aigen Srl
Via Pietrasanta12
20141 Milan
Italy
Tel: +39 02 897 869 22
www.europeanetwork.com

puredistance

Franziskanerplatz 6
1010 Vienna
Austria
Tel. +43 1 513 55 18
info@puredistance.com
www.puredistance.com

ROBERT PIGUET

PARFUMS

16 East 40th Street
Suite 700
New York, NY 10016
USA
Tel: +1 212 840 8800
jgarces@ffandcltd.com
www.robertpiguetparfums.com

ROJA DOVE

HAUTE PARFUMERIE

RDPR
26 Clifton Terrace
Brighton, BN1 3HB
England
Tel: +44 1273 827 430
www.rdprgroup.com
www.rojadove.com

SERGE LUTENS

Harrods
87–135 Brompton Road
London, SW1X 7XL
England
Tel: +44 207 730 1234
www.harrods.com

TEO CABANEL
PARIS

28 rue François Millet
77300 Fontainebleau
France
Tel: +33 1 64 22 84 95
info@teo-cabanel.com
www.teo-cabanel.com

The Beautiful Mind Series Intelligence & Fantasy Vol-1

Lins House
38 Roseberry Avenue
London, EC1R 4RN
England
Tel: Jeff +44 7880 746 289
David +44 7787 500 729
jeff@thiscompany.org, david@thiscompany.org
www.thebeautifulmindseries.com

LUBIN
PARIS

3 Rue du Roule
75001 Paris
France
Tel: +33 1 44 88 95 80
contact@lubin.eu
www.lubin.eu

TOM FORD BEAUTY

www.tomford.com

Van Cleef & Arpels
PARFUMS

Harrods
87–135 Brompton Road
London, SW1X 7XL
England
Tel: +44 207 730 1234
www.harrods.com

.vero.profumo.

Campomarzio 70
Via di Campomarzio 70
00186 ROMA
Italy
Tel: +39 06 6920 2123
info@campomarzio70.it
www.veroprofumo.com

XERJOFF

Oystersin srl
Via Collegno 11
10143 Torino
Italy
Tel: +39 01 1316 7023
about-xj@xerjoff.com, info@oystersin.com
www.xerjoff.com

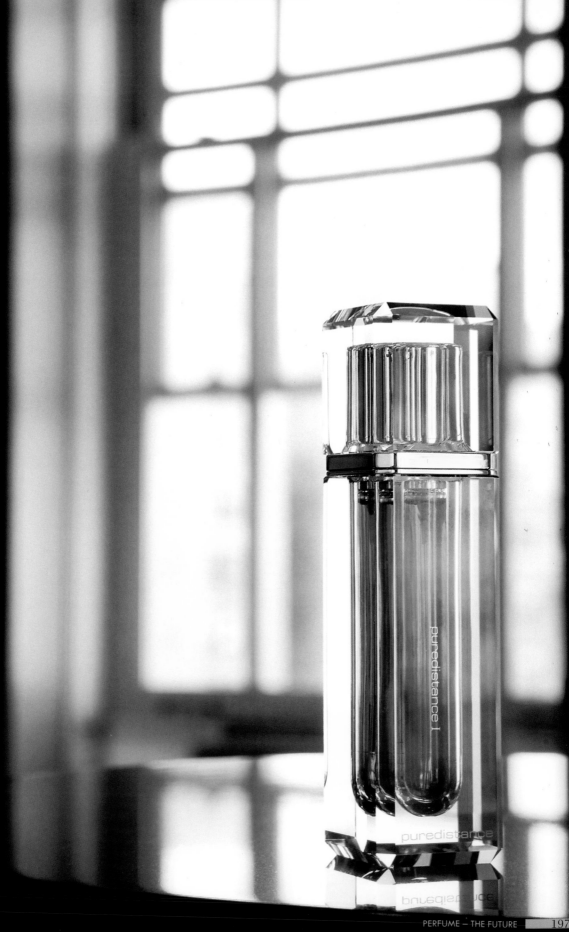